The Kingdom of God
in the
Synoptic Tradition

Richard H. Hiers

University of Florida Press
Gainesville • *1970*

COPYRIGHT © 1970 BY THE STATE OF FLORIDA
DEPARTMENT OF GENERAL SERVICES

LIBRARY OF CONGRESS
CATALOG CARD No. 70-630982
ISBN 0-8130-0305-9

PRINTED BY THE STORTER PRINTING COMPANY
GAINESVILLE, FLORIDA

Preface

TWO CHAPTERS have previously appeared in print, substantially in their present form: Chapter 1 in *JBL* (1966), and Chapter 2 in *JAAR* (1967). I am grateful to the editors of these journals for permission to include this material here. I also wish to thank Professors A. Roy Eckardt, Morton S. Enslin, Floyd V. Filson, and Krister Stendahl for their responses to some of these and related studies.

Teachers often wonder at the strange things their students think they have learned. Consequently, I blame none in particular for the results presented here. Nevertheless, I take this occasion to express appreciation to my former professors of Biblical study: Millar Burrows, Brevard S. Childs, Erich Dinkler, Paul W. Meyer, B. Davie Napier, and Marvin Pope. I remember with special gratitude and joy my teacher and friend, the late Paul Schubert. My thanks go also to many others, fellow students, colleagues, and friends, for their interest and encouragement, especially Austin B. Creel and Delton L. Scudder.

I am glad to acknowledge the assistance which I have received from the University of Florida through Graduate and Humanities Council research grants, the Division of Sponsored Research, and the University of Florida Libraries.

R.H.H.

ABBREVIATIONS

Bauer, *Lexicon*	Walter Bauer, *A Greek-English Lexicon of the New Testament,* ET and ed. by W. F. Arndt and F. W. Gingrich (Chicago, 1957)
Billerbeck	Hermann L. Strack und Paul Billerbeck, *Kommentar zum Neuen Testament aus Talmud und Midrasch* (Munich, 1922–28), 4 vols.
BR	*Biblical Research*
ET	English Translation
HTR	*Harvard Theological Review*
IB	*Interpreter's Bible*
ICC	International Critical Commentary
JAAR	*Journal of the American Academy of Religion*
JBL	*Journal of Biblical Literature*
JBR	*Journal of the Bible and Religion*
JR	*Journal of Religion*
JTS	*Journal of Theological Studies*
LXX	Septuagint
NEB	New English Bible
NT	*Novum Testamentum*
NT	New Testament
NTS	*New Testament Studies*
OT	Old Testament
RGG	*Die Religion in Geschichte und Gegenwart*
RSV	Revised Standard Version
SBT	Studies in Biblical Theology
SJT	*Scottish Journal of Theology*
T&L	*Theology and Life*
ZNW	*Zeitschrift für die neutestamentliche Wissenschaft*

DEAD SEA SCROLLS

IQGA	Genesis Apocryphon
IQH	Hodayoth, or Thanksgiving Psalms
IQM	War Scroll
4QM[a]	War Scroll fragment Cave 4

Contents

Introduction

According to synoptic tradition,[1] the coming of the Kingdom of God was the thematic message of the historical Jesus and the "twelve" apostles or messengers who joined their efforts to his during his lifetime. But what did Jesus and his companions understand the Kingdom of God to mean? The answers given have generally varied with the interests or commitments of those discussing the question. It was only about eighty years ago that critical historians—i.e., those who attempt to weigh the evidence critically or objectively—began to suspect that Jesus may have thought of it in terms of the eschatological[2] beliefs of his Jewish predecessors and contemporaries. There was no single eschatological scheme in first-century Judaism, but there were a number of pervasive motifs: the Age to Come or Messianic Age would be inaugurated by God's intervention in history after, with or without the appearance of a Messiah or messianic figure such as a king from the house of David, "the Son of man," or Elijah; there would be a time of tribulation or suffering, at the end of which Satan would finally be overthrown; the earth would be transformed after the pattern of the garden of Eden, man and nature redeemed from the curse of frustration and death; and the righteous would enter this Kingdom of God on earth and share in the messianic banquet and era, while the unrighteous would forever be excluded from it.

1. The basic evidence is reviewed below, pp. 7–9 and *passim* (see Index of primary citations). The term "synoptic" refers to the first three gospels (Matthew, Mark, Luke) which, when compared or "looked at together," are similar or even identical at numerous places, in contrast to the Fourth Gospel (John) with which the first three have little in common.
2. The term "eschatology" or "eschatological" as used here refers to the conceptions of the events associated in first-century Jewish and Christian thought with the anticipated end of the present age or world, and the coming or beginning on earth of the Kingdom of God or Messianic Age. For further definition, see below, pp. 94 ff.

The two most important proponents of this interpretation published their findings around the turn of the present century: Johannes Weiss and Albert Schweitzer. In their view, the distinctive feature of Jesus' eschatological understanding was his conviction that the time for these decisive events had come near: they would be fulfilled in his own lifetime, or at the latest within the lifetime of some of his contemporaries.

At first, this interpretation was thought too alarming, for it called into question both the liberal Protestant image of Jesus as the teacher of timeless (i.e., modern) truths or ethics, and the Catholic and traditional Protestant equation of the historical Jesus with the divine and omniscient Christ of the Fourth Gospel and subsequent Christian doctrine. With few exceptions, British and American writers preferred to maintain that Jesus did not look for the imminent onset of the Messianic Age. Instead, most held, he believed and proclaimed that it had already come, if only partially. Many used C. H. Dodd's term "realized eschatology" to signify this understanding. After some hesitation, German historians generally came to accept the basic position of Weiss and Schweitzer, at least their consensus that Jesus had expected the arrival of the Kingdom in the near future—thus, for instance, Rudolf Bultmann, Martin Dibelius, Hans Windisch. But in this case, what could Jesus' understanding and message mean to modern men who do not believe that the present world is coming to an end, or that Satan now rules but that God is about to establish His Kingdom on earth? Bultmann proposed that Jesus' understanding and message should be "demythologized," i.e., that the "mythological" (first-century Jewish eschatological) aspects should be re-interpreted (or abandoned!) and the central idea expressed in terms of modern categories. For Bultmann, this meant categories drawn from existentialist philosophy; thus he speaks of Jesus' "understanding of the meaning of existence"[3] as the essential matter.

3. Bultmann and many of his pupils also speak of the understanding of existence expressed in or elicited by the *kerygma*, i.e., the "preaching" or message of the early Church. Bultmann gladly relegates the historical Jesus to first-century Judaism (so far as his significance for theology is concerned), but maintains the essential identity of the early Christian *kerygma* (by which he usually means his rendering of Pauline theology) with the preaching of the Church today. The central issue in the so-called new quest of the historical Jesus is the relationship between Jesus' understanding "of the meaning of existence" and that implicit in the *kerygma*. Proponents of the "new quest" generally wish to sanctify their conception of the *kerygma* or the understanding

Few Anglo-Saxon critics have been willing to accept Dodd's claim that for Jesus the Kingdom was virtually *entirely* present. And few German scholars in or out of Bultmann's circle have continued to hold that Jesus thought it exclusively future. For the past decade or two, the dominant hypothesis has been that the historical Jesus thought and proclaimed that the Kingdom of God was both future and, in some sense, also present.

This hypothesis is subjected to scrutiny in the studies that follow. The tendency of interpreters to circumvent the evidence that Jesus looked for the coming of the Kingdom in the near future is traced to the dogmatic interests or presuppositions of these interpreters (Chapter 1). Since most of the synoptic evidence indicates unambiguously that Jesus and his followers looked for the coming of the Kingdom in the future, attention is focused here upon those passages which have been most often claimed by proponents of the view that Jesus thought the Kingdom present. These are treated exegetically in Chapters 2–4 and 7. Since the significance of Jesus' and his followers' exorcisms figures prominently in analysis of two of these passages (Chapters 3 and 4), the question of the relationship between demon-exorcism and the coming of the Kingdom is pursued further in the exegesis of two other pertinent passages (Chapters 5 and 6). Chapter 8 is devoted to analysis of a saying usually dismissed out of hand by those who suppose that Jesus himself could not have said such a thing.

Admittedly, the task is complicated by the fact that the traditions have come to us through the hands of the early churches and the various evangelists, whose problems and interests may well be represented in the present form of the stories and sayings.[4] The authenticity of the traditions cannot simply be assumed. Moreover, many of the passages to be examined are notoriously "difficult." Our contention, however, is that much of such "difficulty" arises out of unwillingness on the part of interpreters to take seriously Jesus' eschatological outlook.

These exegetical studies and a review of the parables (Chapter

---

"of the meaning of existence" imputed to it by finding its parallel or basis in the historical Jesus.

4. For an introduction to the types of literary analysis known as form criticism and redaction criticism, see, respectively, Rudolf Bultmann and Karl Kundsin, *Form Criticism* (New York, 1962), and Willi Marxsen, *Mark the Evangelist: Studies on the Redaction History of the Gospel* (Nashville, 1969).

9) indicate fairly clearly that Jesus regarded the coming of the Kingdom as a future, supernatural occurrence. That he thought it present on earth in any sense is doubtful.

It is equally unlikely that any of the synoptic evangelists or their "sources" (Mark, "Q," "M," and "L")[5] thought that the Kingdom of God was yet present or had been present on earth (Chapter 10). For the historical Jesus and the synoptic tradition alike, the Kingdom of God was still to come. The fact that this expectation was fulfilled neither in that generation nor any subsequent to date does not alter the evidence that Jesus and the early Christian community looked for its actualization in the near future.

It is ironic that this problem which was pivotal to the "quest of the historical Jesus," the "realized eschatology" debate, the "demythologizing controversy," and to the whole course of NT study in this century has largely escaped the attention of the nonspecialist. Laymen generally suppose that the real problem about the historical Jesus is whether he really existed, at least as described in the gospel traditions;[6] or whether the Dead Sea Scrolls discredit him as a mere echo of the Qumran Teacher of Righteousness; or whether Schonfield (or any other popularizer) has at last proven him some kind of fanatic or political operator.[7] These misplaced or spurious concerns have, in part, been fed by the desire of authors and publishers to sell print. But they also result from the failure of NT specialists to expose to public view (and often to their own awareness) the specifically eschatological nature of Jesus' beliefs and preaching indicated in the synoptic tradition.

5. It is widely recognized that Matthew and Luke both utilized Mark for their narrative framework and certain other material. Sayings that appear in approximately the same form in Matthew and Luke but not occurring in Mark are designated by the letter "Q" for the German *Quelle*, meaning "source." Whether such a "source" was oral or written, or even existed, are other questions. The letter "M" designates material found only in Matthew, and "L" what is peculiar to Luke. Some of the "M" or "L" traditions may have come from "Q"; these letters may also include several different subsources and material authored by the evangelists themselves.

6. Few critical scholars, of course, would claim that the Jesus portrayed in the Fourth Gospel corresponds to the Jesus of history. By no means all of the synoptic tradition is to be taken as evidence for the historical Jesus either; but here, at least, there is much that can be so regarded with a high degree of probability, as even so radical a critic as Rudolf Bultmann concedes (*Jesus and the Word* [New York, 1958], p. 14).

7. On J. M. Allegro and H. J. Schonfield, see Otto Betz, "The Crisis in N.T. Theology: The Gap between the Historical Jesus and the Faith of the Church," Chicago Theological Seminary *Register* 59 (1969), esp. pp. 12–16.

However strange this outlook may seem to us, it is quite characteristic of first-century Judaism and Christianity, and constitutes a basic feature of the context in which the latter developed. Perhaps the present study can serve to introduce the nonspecialist to, and remind the specialist of the eschatological character of, the Kingdom of God in the synoptic tradition, a factor which must be recognized if one wishes even to begin to comprehend the intention and activity of the historical Jesus and the early Christian community.

1

Eschatology and Methodology

A S ALBERT SCHWEITZER and more recently others also have shown, the efforts on the part of NT scholars and others prior to 1900 to portray the life and teaching of Jesus were by and large highly subjective and fanciful. In nearly every case, these writers managed to delineate a Jesus in modern dress, devoted to the concerns of modern men, and lending the weight of his good name to their causes—e.g., the furtherance of rational religion, the triumph of the proletariat, the fulfillment of man's progress toward the perfect society on earth.[1] Jesus had apparently been doing well in these modernizing schools, and was advancing toward graduation into the world of respectable, contemporary society. But just when everything was going so well, it was discovered, to nearly everyone's dismay—including that of the two principal discoverers, Johannes Weiss and Albert Schweitzer—that the modern (late nineteenth-century) Jesus was a figment of liberal theology's imagination: that the historical Jesus is "to our time a stranger and an enigma," who returns to his own time.[2] So long as Jesus' eschatological outlook was ignored, it seemed possible, by use of only moderately ingenious exegetics, to find in him the advocate of all sorts of modern-day viewpoints and concerns. But once his eschatological outlook was recognized, it was no longer so easy to claim his endorsement.

It is not surprising that many writers since Schweitzer have been

1. Schweitzer's *The Quest of the Historical Jesus* (New York, 1950) is still the best summary of these efforts. He writes, retrospectively, of the eighteenth- and nineteenth-century "lives" of Jesus, "Thus each successive epoch of theology found its own thoughts in Jesus. . . . But it was not only each epoch that found its reflection in Jesus; each individual created Him in accordance with his own character" (p. 4). These words were also prophetic of many of the treatments yet to come. See also Gösta Lundström, *The Kingdom of God in the Teaching of Jesus* (Richmond, 1963), Chs. 1–3, 9–11.

2. Schweitzer, *Quest*, p. 399.

6

unwilling to surrender their versions of the "historical" Jesus without a struggle. What more powerful ally could one have on behalf of his particular cause than "the Founder" (as many liberal writers preferred to call Jesus) himself? Furthermore, many modern Christian exegetes and moralists remained convinced that Jesus' message—his gospel and ethics—is still authoritative for and relevant to the Christian life today. Given this conviction, surely Jesus must have intended his message for our day, and not simply for his own generation.[3] Furthermore, the eschatological interpretation of Jesus' outlook and teaching seemed to undermine his authority: if Jesus were mistaken about the time of the coming of the kingdom of God, then perhaps he was in error about some other things as well, such as his relationship to God or the nature of the moral life.[4]

By far the clearest and most forceful and, incidentally, the first thorough analysis of the synoptic evidence apropos of Jesus' concept of the kingdom of God is the first edition of Johannes Weiss' *Die Predigt Jesu vom Reiche Gottes,* a slender volume of which Rudolf Bultmann says, "This epoch-making book refuted the interpretation which was hitherto generally accepted. Weiss showed that the Kingdom of God is not immanent in the world and does not grow as part of the world's history, but is rather eschatological; i.e., the Kingdom of God transcends the historical order. It will come into being not through the moral endeavour of man, but solely through the supernatural action of God. God will suddenly put an end to the world and to history, and He will bring in a new world, the world of eternal blessedness."[5] Since this book is now to be available in English, a brief summary of Weiss' argument will suffice.

The eschatological character of Jesus' Galilean preaching, Weiss suggests, is evidenced not only in Mark 1 : 15 and Matt. 4 : 17, "Repent; the kingdom of God is at hand," but also in the "Q" summaries which in their earliest form describe Jesus as "preaching

3. This conviction has been a major factor in the resistance of many writers to Schweitzer's characterization of Jesus' message as "an ethic for the interim." See my article "Interim Ethics," *T&L* 9 (1966), 220–33.

4. E.g., George E. Ladd, *Jesus and the Kingdom* (New York, 1964), pp. 136 f.

5. *Jesus Christ and Mythology* (New York, 1958), p. 12. See also the appraisal of Weiss by David Larrimore Holland, "History, Theology and the Kingdom of God," *BR* 13 (1968), 1–13.

the gospel of the kingdom saying: Repent" (Matt. 4 : 23, 9 : 35; Luke 4 : 43, 8 : 1). He instructs his disciples to proclaim this same message as he sends them on their preaching mission (Matt. 10 : 7; Luke 10 : 9, 11): "The meaning of this well-attested proclamation of Jesus and his disciples seems quite clear: the kingdom (or the rule) of God has drawn so near that it stands at the door. Therefore, while the *basileia* (Kingdom) is not yet *here*, it is extremely near."[6]

The first supplication of the prayer Jesus put on the lips of his disciples, Weiss points out, was "Thy kingdom come!" "The meaning is not 'may thy kingdom grow,' 'may thy kingdom be perfected,' but, rather, 'may thy kingdom *come*.' *For the disciples*, the *basileia* is not yet here, not even in its beginnings; therefore Jesus bids them: *zēteite tēn basileian* (seek the Kingdom) (Luke 12 : 31). This yearning and longing for its coming, this ardent prayer for it, and the constant hope that it will come—that it will come soon— this is their religion." Only the Father knows when the kingdom will come; there is no way to calculate the time of its arrival—not even the Son knows that (Mark 13 : 32), but Jesus' followers can be sure that God will bring it (Luke 12 : 32; 18 : 7 f.; 21 : 28).

Nevertheless, Jesus expected the kingdom to come in the very near future. His instructions to his disciples as he sent them on their preaching mission (Matt. 10 : 5 ff.; Luke 10 : 10 f.) make sense only when we realize that in Jesus' view no time was to be lost: " . . . in case a town should not receive them, they were immediately and emphatically to abandon all further attempts to approach it and were to shake off its dust from their feet. Such a procedure is anything but 'pastoral.' . . . It can only be explained on the supposition that no time may be lost with fruitless or problematical efforts. Where they meet with unresponsiveness, no more energy dare be wasted there which might better be directed toward receptive souls. The expectation of the *immediate* onset of the end forms the background for these ideas."

At some point, however, Jesus began to realize that the kingdom would not come during his own lifetime. But he still expected it to come during the lifetime of the generation of his contemporaries (Mark 13 : 30 and par.). In Mark 9 : 43 ff. it "is presupposed that

6. *Die Predigt Jesu vom Reiche Gottes* (Göttingen, 1892), p. 12. The following pages of the same work are also cited in the discussion which follows: 17, 25, 27, 36 f., 42, 49, 63, 65–67.

those to whom the words are addressed will *live to see* the coming of the kingdom," but first they must pass through the final Judgment. At the time of Judgment, the dead, having been raised, including even those of ancient and foreign cities and nations, will pass before the judgment throne of the Son of man, where the fate of each will be decided: those found righteous will then enter the kingdom of God and sit at messianic table in the bright warm banquet hall with the patriarchs (Matt. 8 : 11 f.), while the wicked will suffer exclusion from the kingdom of God.

At the Last Supper, Jesus made it plain to his disciples that he would not again drink of the fruit of the vine until the kingdom of God had come (Luke 22 : 18). But to the meek, he promised that they would inherit the kingdom (Matt. 5 : 5). When Jesus spoke of "possessing" or "entering" the kingdom of God, he meant, as in the Beatitudes generally, the assurance of participation, and even, perhaps, bearing rule in the kingdom of God at that time *in the future* when God brings it. The kingdom will belong only to those who by repentance (*metanoia*) have made themselves ready for it. Weiss does not use Schweitzer's term, "interim ethic" or "ethic for the interim," but his interpretation is virtually identical at this point: "The 'righteousness of the kingdom of God' does not signify the ethical perfection which members of the kingdom possess or achieve *in* the kingdom of God, but rather the *dikaiosunē* (righteousness) which is the *condition for entrance into* the kingdom of God (Matt. 5 : 20)." One must be prepared to give up everything else for the sake of this highest, ultimate Good, as the parables of the pearl and the treasure in the field make very plain.[7]

Weiss was quite aware that recognizing the eschatological character of Jesus' conception of the kingdom of God would make it no longer possible to maintain that the words and outlook of the historical Jesus and the late-nineteenth-century theological interpretation of Jesus and his message were one and the same. He insists, therefore, that ". . . we cannot any longer use Jesus' words in the exact sense that was originally intended."

Weiss noted that his conclusions "present peculiar difficulties for systematic and practical theology"; in particular, the Protestant liberal understanding that the kingdom of God could be interpreted "as an 'actualization of the rule of God' by human ethical

7. Matt. 13 : 44–46. See also Luke 12 : 31; Matt. 6 : 31.

activity" is now seen to be not only without support from the historical Jesus, but "completely contrary to the transcendentalism of Jesus' idea."

What, then, should theology do? It not only could, but should, Weiss urged, retain the concept "kingdom of God" as "the characteristic watchword of modern theology. *Only the admission must be demanded that we use it in a different sense from Jesus'*."

Albert Schweitzer's interpretation of Jesus' eschatological message and ministry is generally more familiar than Weiss' and need not be summarized here. It may simply be noted that Schweitzer arrived independently at very much the same conclusions as Weiss, setting down his position initially in his "Sketch of the Life of Jesus,"[8] and with some further additions in his celebrated, though often misread, *Quest of the Historical Jesus*.[9] Like Weiss, Schweitzer did not shrink from concluding that the historical, eschatological Jesus is "a stranger and an enigma" to our time, and that, accordingly, "the historical foundation of Christianity as built up by rationalistic, by liberal, and by modern theology no longer exists."[10]

Both Weiss and Schweitzer were concerned to show how this strange, eschatological Jesus with his negative, world-renouncing ethic might nevertheless be understood to mean something for our own time.[11] Their proposals may have some merit, even though a considerable gap remains between the historical Jesus of their exegesis and the Jesus they found relevant to the modern world. The point to be noted here is that both men were capable of differentiating between the descriptive, historical-critical task and the theological, interpretative task. They did not allow themselves to be forced off the road of straightforward historical exegesis by fear or hallucinations of on-coming theological "difficulties."

Some of the more recent studies of the Kingdom of God in the synoptic tradition have not proceeded so forthrightly. In many of them the methodology employed seems to proceed on the principle that the end justifies the means. The implicit end is to get rid of

8. ET, *The Mystery of the Kingdom of God* (New York, 1950).

9. Schweitzer's most recent account of Jesus' ministry and message was written in 1951: *The Kingdom of God and Primitive Christianity* (New York, 1968), esp. pp. 68–130. His position basically is the same here as in his earlier studies.   10. *Quest*, p. 399.

11. For analysis of Schweitzer's suggestions, see my book *Jesus and Ethics* (Philadelphia, 1968), Chapter 2.

Jesus' strange, eschatological ideas and, with them, the attendant theological "difficulties" that seem to stand between him and his significance "for us" today.[12] To achieve such a worthy goal, surely any means or methodology—if necessary, several at the same time —will do! Diverse as many of these studies are as to specific theological interest, it will be seen that they are guided by the same methodological consideration: to *dispose of* the eschatological aspects of Jesus' thought, preaching, and activity.

Perhaps the simplest method is that demonstrated in B. H. Branscomb, *The Teaching of Jesus.* Here the author simply ignores the eschatological evidence, and so finds no difficulty in presenting Jesus as founder of the "kingdom of the heart," a moral philosopher enunciating virtues and great principles for all generations to come. Various writers, such as C. H. Dodd, strategically by-pass inconvenient synoptic texts; for instance, Dodd nowhere accounts for Matt. 10 : 23 or Luke 10 : 12.[13] T. W. Manson ignores a whole series of passages that are contrary to his thesis that in the latter phase of his ministry Jesus thought in terms of "realized eschatology."[14] Karl Adam notes that the eschatological interpretation makes much of Mark 9 : 1, 13 : 30, and par., and promises "an unprejudiced evaluation" of these texts, but then never mentions them again.[15] But usually, as in the case of Dodd and Manson, this method is relied upon only in conjunction with other, more sophisticated methods.

E. F. Scott presents a variation: in his earliest study of synoptic eschatology, *The Kingdom and the Messiah,* he was still under the influence of Schweitzer's view that for Jesus the Kingdom of God was entirely future and imminent; but in his later books, he seems to have forgotten (though he does not explicitly repudiate) that understanding, and therefore feels free to describe Jesus as the teacher of permanently valid moral principles, who meant by the term "kingdom of God" only the life of "inward fellowship with God."[16]

12. Thus, e.g., Heinz Zahrnt, *The Historical Jesus* (New York, 1963), p. 53; Hermann Schuster, "Die Konsequente Eschatologie in der Interpretation des Neuen Testaments, Kritisch Betrachtet," ZNW 47 (1956), 22.

13. See Lundström, *Kingdom of God,* p. 121.

14. For instance, Mark 10 : 23, 14 : 25 (=Luke 22 : 18); Luke 10 : 9, 11; 12 : 35–48; 19 : 11–26.

15. *The Christ of Faith* (New York, 1960), p. 314.

16. *The Kingdom of God in the New Testament* (New York, 1931), p. 186.

Another method is to suggest that some, at least, of the eschatological sayings attributed to Jesus were really put into his mouth by the early church or the evangelists. An early exemplar of this position is George B. Stevens of Yale University, who notes the tendency of preachers and exegetes to evade the plain eschatological meaning of the synoptic texts: "One can only wonder whether [this procedure] could ever have obtained the consent and advocacy of candid men in any other realm than that of theology."[17] But then Stevens goes on to claim that this plain eschatological teaching was improperly attributed to Jesus by the apostolic church. Evidently it was all right for the church to be mistaken, but not for Jesus to be! Few critics attempt to attribute *all* of the eschatological passages to the church, but some, for instance, Hans Windisch and C. H. Dodd, intimate that quite a number of them may be eliminated in this manner.[18] It is interesting to notice that a Roman Catholic writer may feel that he is denied this option. "The most immediate explanation of this difficulty would be that the Evangelists, imprisoned in the errors of their age, had read their own false views into Jesus' words; it might be assumed that the error was not the Lord's doing, but the Evangelists'. But this interpretation cannot be reconciled with the dogma of inspiration."[19] One can appreciate the dilemma of the scholar who wishes to undertake an "unprejudiced evaluation" of the text, but within the limits set by the dogma of an infallible Jesus on one hand, and that of an infallible Bible on the other.

A different line of interpretation is followed by those who state, in effect, that Jesus talked in terms of the eschatological ideas of his contemporaries, but only out of deference to their limited understanding and that in fact he actually meant something else. This method assumes that Jesus did not really share the eschatological outlook of his contemporaries, but used its terminology to convey to them fragments of a truth which they were incapable of understanding in noneschatological categories. Thus E. F. Scott speaks of Jesus' eschatological language as a "vehicle" for his thought. This language was only symbolic, "little more than figura-

17. "Is There a Self-consistent New Testament Eschatology?" *American Journal of Theology* 6 (1902), 67.
18. Windisch, *The Meaning of the Sermon on the Mount* (Philadelphia, 1950), p. 26; C. H. Dodd, *The Parables of the Kingdom*, rev. ed. (New York, 1961), pp. 138 f.
19. Adam, *The Christ of Faith*, p. 320.

tive." "Yet in the last resort (Jesus) has broken with the apocalyptic view," and really understood the kingdom of God as "a fact of the inward life," or "fellowship with God."[20]

C. H. Dodd describes Jesus' eschatological imagery as intended only to symbolize "the moral universe," or "the eternal realities," or an "order beyond space and time."[21] Amos Wilder speaks of Jesus' references to the eschatological kingdom of God as "stylistic," or symbolic of "ineffable" realities, or as intended to dramatize his message to "simple people."[22] Even Bultmann, who usually gives the impression of knowing better, sometimes describes Jesus as having been *first* an existentialist preacher of the Will of God, and only afterwards an eschatologist. Eschatology was only "mythology," the "garments" in which "the real meaning in Jesus' teaching finds its outward expression," viz., "that man *now* stands under the necessity of decision, that his 'Now' is always for him the last hour."[23]

Bultmann reveals his failure to comprehend the reality and significance for Jesus of the coming eschatological event in his embarrassment over the theological or moral problem of eschatological "rewards" in Jesus' teaching. Bultmann writes as if there were something extraneous or unseemly (at any rate, un-Lutheran) about Jesus' attaching the promise (or threat) of eschatological rewards (or punishment) to his proclamation of God's demand for radical obedience.[24] He fails to grasp that if Jesus really believed that the Kingdom of God, the Son of man, and the Judgment were near—whether in a few weeks or a few years—it would not have been a question of "rewards," but of responding in the face of this decisive event in such a way as to have some hope of surviving Judgment and entering the Kingdom. This Kingdom is coming. Will men be found penitent, faithful, fit for entering it? Bultmann puts the cart

20. *Kingdom of God*, pp. 82, 95; cf. p. 110.

21. *The Gospel in the New Testament* (London, n.d.), p. 29; *Parables*, pp. 40, 83. For a critique of Dodd see C. C. McCown, "Symbolic Interpretation," *JBL* 63 (1944), 335–38.

22. *Eschatology and Ethics in the Teaching of Jesus* (New York, 1950), pp. 60, 89, 113. For appraisal of Wilder, see C. Freeman Sleeper, "Some American Contributions to New Testament Interpretation," *Interpretation* 20 (1966), 329–37.

23. *Jesus and the Word*, pp. 55 f., 131; "Jesus and Paul," in *Existence and Faith* (New York, 1960), p. 186. See also Paul Schubert, "The Synoptic Gospels and Eschatology," *JBR* 14 (1946), 156.

24. *Jesus and the Word*, pp. 79, 121; *Theology of the New Testament*, I (New York, 1954), pp. 14 f.

before the horse when he describes Jesus as demanding radical obedience and *then*, in order to motivate compliance with this radical ethic of neighbor-love, adding the sanctions of rewards and punishments. Bultmann falls into the trap described by Schweitzer in 1901: "So long as one starts with the ethics and seeks to comprehend the eschatology as something adventitious, there appears to be no organic connection between the two."[25] Wilder's distinction between "formal" and "essential" sanctions similarly begins with Jesus' ethics, but ends in a disjunction between ethics and eschatology.

Several writers feel that the eschatological interpretation—and with it, presumably, the eschatological passages it explains—should be disposed of more emphatically. The tone is that of indignation. The method is that of sarcasm or *reductio ad absurdum*. The presupposition is that Jesus had divine foreknowledge of the future, or, at any rate, was not so unreasonable (i.e., so unlike us) as actually to have "swallowed uncritically the contents of the Jewish messianic hope."[26] "Even if Jesus used at times some of the imagery of the apocalyptists, and even though he shares some of their underlying ideas, yet He never identified the Kingdom of God with any of these *dreams*."[27] Jesus could not possibly have been guided by what to us is so obviously a "fantastic delusion."[28] Nothing about the Sermon on the Mount has the "burning odour of the cosmic catastrophy," writes Bornkamm.[29] Schweitzer is often accused of having described Jesus as "fanatical" or "deluded";[30] hence his interpretation can be readily dismissed, since Jesus, whether seen from the perspective of conservative or liberal theology, *of course*, was not deluded! Schweitzer nowhere describes

25. *Mystery*, pp. 51 f.
26. T. W. Manson, "Realized Eschatology and the Messianic Secret," in G. E. Nineham (ed.), *Studies in the Gospels* (Oxford, 1955), p. 210.
27. Dodd, *Gospel*, p. 19 (ital. mine).
28. Adam, *The Christ of Faith*, p. 67. See the review of such interpretations in Norman Perrin, *The Kingdom of God in the Teaching of Jesus* (Philadelphia, 1963), pp. 51, 150.
29. Günther Bornkamm, *Jesus of Nazareth* (London, 1960), p. 223. See Leander E. Keck's excellent criticism, "Bornkamm's *Jesus of Nazareth* Revisited," *JR* 49 (1969), esp. pp. 11 f.
30. E.g., Hugh Anderson, "The Historical Jesus and the Origins of Christianity," *SJT* 13 (1960), 13; James Kallas, *Jesus and the Power of Satan* (Philadelphia, 1968), p. 69; Howard C. Kee, *Jesus in History* (New York, 1970), pp. 17 f.

Jesus as a fanatic or "deluded," however, and in his M.D. disserta-
tion, *Die psychiatrische Beurteilung Jesu,* points out numerous
fundamental errors, both historical-critical and psychoanalytical,
in certain interpretations which so described Jesus.

Another method used in attacking the eschatological meaning
can be designated simply as devious or forced exegesis. For example, Herman Ridderbos, noting the unfavorable connotation of
the term "this generation," concludes, speaking of Mark 13 : 30 and
par., that "we *must not* attribute a temporal meaning" to these
words, but rather "must conceive of it" as referring to people of any
age whose "disposition and frame of mind . . . are averse to Jesus
and his words." Similarly, he argues that Matt. 23 : 39 (Luke
13 : 35) and Mark 14 : 62 (Matt. 26 : 64) are to be thought of as
addressed to the Jewish people and their leaders generally, "without inferring . . . that the latter would witness the *parousia* of the
Son of Man before their deaths."[31]

A classic example of devious exegesis is C. H. Dodd's proposed
translation and interpretation of Mark 9 : 1. "The bystanders are
not promised that they shall see the Kingdom of God *coming,* but
that they shall come to see that the Kingdom of God *has already
come,* at some point before they became aware of it."[32] Perrin
furnishes a similar instance of eisegesis: of the petition "Thy kingdom come," he writes, "we must remember that those who are
being taught to use this petition are those for whom the Kingdom
is already a matter of personal experience. They are therefore
either being taught to pray that others may share this experience;
or, more probably, they are being taught to pray for the consummation of that which has begun within their experience."[33]

A more subtle type of methodology is pursued by most of the
more recent NT critics, who concede that Jesus both talked eschatologically and really meant what he said; and yet, in one way or
another, they undertake to show that Jesus really meant something else *as well* in speaking of the Kingdom, and that the

31. *The Coming of the Kingdom* (Philadelphia, 1962), pp. 502 f.
32. *Parables,* p. 37n1. This interpretation is reflected in the NEB's translation of Mark 9 : 1. NEB translators also show a penchant for realized eschatology in rendering several other verses, e.g., Matt. 12 : 28 = Luke 11 : 20;
Mark 1 : 15; Matt. 3 : 2, 4 : 17, 10 : 7, 21 : 31; Luke 17 : 21. The director of
the NEB Committee was C. H. Dodd! See below, p. 82n7.
33. *Kingdom of God,* p. 193.

modern reader should pay attention only to that something else. Tacitly they permit the eschatological Kingdom of God to fall into the background, and, if possible, drop completely out of sight.

Harnack develops the prototype of this method in his *Das Wesen des Christentums.*[34] Jesus did share the eschatological outlook of his contemporaries, Harnack admits, but at the same time held a radically different notion about the essential meaning of the Kingdom of God. To him, it really meant personal religious experience: "God and the soul; the soul and its God," the "Rule of God in the hearts of men." How did Jesus manage to hold such irreconcilable notions simultaneously? Harnack's answer was straightforward if incredible: Jesus simply failed to perceive the contradiction, though it is obvious to us. We should think only of what was "peculiar" or essential in Jesus' message, and forget the "dramatic" and "external" aspects which he "simply shared with his contemporaries." "From this point of view," the eschatological understanding of the Kingdom of God "has *vanished.*"[35] The essence of this procedure is to permit one's eyes to focus only upon the noneschatological meaning attributed to Jesus' words about the Kingdom of God. After a while one will hardly even notice the theologically inconvenient, eschatological Kingdom of God. It simply vanishes, or "pales into insignificance."[36]

Hans Windisch utilizes this kind of methodology in his study on *The Sermon on the Mount.* He grants that Jesus expected the imminent coming of the kingdom of God. But at the same time, Windisch points to a class of proverbial or "wisdom" sayings of Jesus, which make no explicit reference to impending eschatological events. These sayings were not conditioned by Jesus' eschatological outlook, and so are to be regarded, along with such other sayings as can be freed from the eschatological context, as *laws* to be obeyed literally by Christians in all ages. Windisch does not even find any particular difficulty in regarding the eschatologically conditioned sayings as laws for the modern Christian life. Jesus may have meant them for his own generation in the interim before the coming of the kingdom of God; but Windisch does not hesi-

34. ET, *What is Christianity?* (New York, 1957).

35. *Ibid.*, pp. 54 ff. (ital. mine).

36. Adam, *The Christ of Faith*, p. 316. Though a conservative Catholic theologian, Adam's treatment of Jesus' eschatological understanding often resembles Harnack's.

tate to regard them as intended for the modern Christian as well.[37] Windisch then poses for himself the artificial task of constructing from various "hints" contained in the Sermon on the Mount a theory as to how Christians, who are required by Jesus to obey his impossible laws, may nevertheless hope for salvation. In effect, he ignores the eschatological context of Jesus' sayings, both by isolating certain noneschatological sayings, and by regarding all the others as well as "intended for" the present age. He sees Jesus as the giver of eternally valid *laws*, whereas Harnack sees him as the discoverer and advocate of certain timeless or eternally valid ideas or values. The methodology, however, is substantially the same.

Rather than maintain that Jesus held simultaneously that the kingdom of God was future and imminent, and at the same time present and immanent, T. W. Manson suggests that during the early part of his ministry, Jesus thought of it as future; but then, after Peter's recognizing him at Caesarea Philippi as the Christ, Jesus began to speak of it as present, both in his own person and ministry and as the "Reign of God," a "personal relation between God and the individual" which men could enter at any time, rather than as an event or place in time or space.[38] But Manson can maintain his two-phase theory only by ignoring the numerous references to the future and imminent appearance of the kingdom of God which are to be found in the synoptic tradition *following* Caesarea Philippi.

Furthermore, Manson is unwilling to permit the conclusion that Jesus could actually have been mistaken in proclaiming the kingdom of God as a coming eschatological event even during the early part of his ministry, and often writes as if Jesus regarded the kingdom of God as present throughout the whole of his ministry.

Amos Wilder, like Harnack and Manson, proposes that Jesus regarded the kingdom of God both as a future eschatological event, and as present in his own person and ministry. And like theirs, Wilder's "both-and" is ultimately reduced to an "either-or": he quietly forgets about the future-eschatological conception, and leaves the reader, in the final analysis, with only realized eschatology. "Interim ethics" is eliminated in favor of "the ethics of the realized kingdom of God."

Perhaps the most popular recent variation on Harnack's method-

---

37. *Sermon on the Mount,* pp. 101, 172 ff.
38. *The Teaching of Jesus* (Cambridge, 1951), pp. 124–29, 135.

ology for disposing of Jesus' futuristic eschatological outlook proceeds with the assertion that, for Jesus, time had no real significance. It is not surprising to find the British Platonist proponent of realized eschatology, C. H. Dodd, arguing: "There is no coming of the Son of Man in history 'after' His coming in Galilee and Jerusalem, whether soon or late, for there is no before and after in the eternal order. The Kingdom of God in its full reality is not something which will happen after other things have happened."[39] It is strange that Bultmann describes Jesus as maintaining that the necessity of decision is the "essential characteristic" of humanity, that "every hour is the last hour." This being the case, "we can understand that for Jesus the whole contemporary mythology is pressed into the service of this conception of human existence."[40] Other theologians, including Hans Conzelmann, have followed Bultmann's lead in trying to eliminate the category of time (and thus also futuristic eschatology) from Jesus' outlook.[41]

Another recent statement of this position is provided by Heinz Zahrnt: "So closely is the coming of the Kingdom of God bound up with the appearance of Jesus that there is 'no more time' between his present proclamation and the final dawning of the Kingdom. There is no room for any further event or any other saving figure."[42] From this perspective, one might say with Harnack, the eschatological understanding "has vanished." But however worthy the motives of these interpreters may be, their declaration that for Jesus and his disciples time had no meaning is guided entirely by dogmatic considerations and is not supported by the synoptic evidence.

The fact that many of the recent studies in synoptic eschatology generally tend toward the elimination or de-emphasizing of the eschatological kingdom of God is a sure sign of dogmatic interest. The studies by Kümmel, Ridderbos, Lundström, Perrin, and Ladd are, for the most part, straightforward, historical-critical examinations of the synoptic evidence and extremely useful critical summaries of the ways in which it has been interpreted since Weiss' monumental volume appeared in 1892. All five find that some of the synoptic texts unmistakably show that Jesus thought of the kingdom of God as a future eschatological event, but that other

39. *Parables*, p. 83.
40. *Jesus and the Word*, pp. 51 f.
41. E.g., Hans Conzelmann, "Jesus Christus," *RGG*[3] III (1959), 644. See Lundström, *Kingdom of God*, pp. 127 ff.
42. *Historical Jesus*, p. 113.

synoptic passages point toward the conclusion that Jesus *also* thought of the kingdom of God as in some sense already present. There is nothing devious in the methodology of these recent studies up to this point.

But then toward the last chapter or in the last part of a decisive chapter[43] even these writers begin to intimate that the significance of Jesus' teaching should, after all, be seen primarily in the sense of its present reality. Here, the significance perceived seems to vary directly with the theological and philosophical commitments of the interpreter. For Ridderbos, Jesus' conception of the present kingdom of God comes out inextricably associated with christology;[44] for Perrin, with "religious experience."[45] It has been noted that for Bultmann, Jesus' eschatological preaching comes down to the proclamation of the eternal "Now" of decision.

In terms of methodology, many of the studies written since 1900 have shown little improvement over Harnack's. True, they do not suppose that the eschatological interpretation and evidence can be disposed of as quickly or completely as Harnack did. What is basically different is that instead of seeing a Protestant "liberal" face at the bottom of the well of history, each sees in the historical Jesus the reflection of his own particular theological milieu: Manson and Dodd, a benign (British) Platonic moralist; Ridderbos, a moderately conservative (Dutch) Evangelical christologist; Bultmann, a (Lutheran) existentialist moral theologian. Everyone forces the kingdom of God violently into his own theological tradition.

The fundamental methodological error in a great many studies of synoptic eschatology in this century has been to begin and proceed with the assumption—sometimes perhaps not even recognized—that one must, somehow or other, *dispose* of the evidence that Jesus thought and spoke of the kingdom of God as a coming

43. W. G. Kümmel, *Promise and Fulfilment*, SBT no. 23 (London, 1957), pp. 151–55; Perrin, *Kingdom of God*, pp. 185 ff.; Ladd, *Jesus and the Kingdom*, pp. 144, 213. Even Lundström, who insists that "The Kingdom of God is absolutely eschatological" and that its "purely future quality . . . should be clearly emphasized" (*Kingdom of God*, pp. 232 f.), concludes that for Jesus and the faithful who see it concentrated but hidden in Jesus, his sayings and miracles, the Kingdom of God has *come*. What is yet to come is not the Kingdom of God, but its "power and glory" (*ibid.*, pp. 234 f., 238).

44. *Coming of the Kingdom*, pp. xxv, 76, 127, 230, 232, 527.

45. *Kingdom of God*, pp. 186, 190 ff., 203.

eschatological event.[46] A variety of devious procedures, calculated in some way or another to eliminate or obscure the eschatological character of Jesus' preaching and outlook, seem to follow inevitably in the wake of this basic a priori error. This error itself seems to stem from two sources. On the one hand, there is the desire to avoid the theological difficulties (whether for liberal or conservative faith) supposedly inherent in the eschatological interpretation: for instance, the possibility that Jesus was limited or mistaken in his knowledge of the future course of history, that he might *not* have intended his teaching as a series of ethical principles or ideals for the guidance of men during all following centuries, or his church as a permanent institution. Since Jesus' teaching and his church are perceived by the Christian to be sources of direction for the life of the Christian community today, it seems much more reasonable to suppose that Jesus intended them to be so.

A second source of error seems to arise out of the desire to achieve a consistent or unitary, rather than an equivocal, conclusion to the question. Since the proponents of the view that Jesus thought of the kingdom of God as both future event *and* present reality have nothing very satisfactory to suggest by way of explaining how the kingdom of God could have been for Jesus both present and *at the same time* future, it seems more reasonable or logical to retain the one and explain away the other (or simply forget about it). Thus the methodologically sound "both-and" is reduced to the seemingly logical or more consistent present or realized eschatology by an act of legerdemain.[47] It is significant that what is usually disposed of is the theologically embarrassing *futuristic* evidence, while the relatively scanty and problematical evidence which might be construed in favor of "realized" eschatology is given full play.

46. There have been notable exceptions, of course: besides Weiss and Schweitzer, there are Walter E. Bundy, Millar Burrows, Martin Dibelius, Morton S. Enslin, Robert M. Grant, Erich Grässer, A. H. M'Neile, W. Manson, and Krister Stendahl, to name only some of the most prominent.

47. Of those critics who maintain a "both-and" position, Kümmel does so most successfully: *Promise and Fulfilment*; "Futuristic and Realized Eschatology in the Earliest Stages of Christianity," *JR* 43 (1963), 303–14. But the precise sense in which Kümmel understands Jesus to have thought the Kingdom present is unclear. This difficulty obtains also in Bornkamm, *Jesus*, and Zahrnt, *Historical Jesus*. Balance is maintained fairly well also by Floyd V. Filson, "The Kingdom; Present and Future," *JBR* 7 (1939), 59–63, and Rudolf Otto, *The Kingdom of God and the Son of Man* (London, 1943).

What is suggested here is only the obvious: the need for distinguishing between the historical-critical task of describing Jesus' conception of the kingdom of God, and the theological task of interpreting the difficulties raised by historical criticism and indicating the way or ways in which the Jesus of history, his ideas, words, and deeds, may mean something for the life of faith in the modern world. When the critical task is carried out with too much concern for the theological difficulties that may result, the temptation arises to make the theological task less difficult by eliminating —through seemingly critical analysis—some of the offending evidence.

In the following exegetical studies attention will be confined to the former task. It may be implied here that theology has some unfinished business on its agenda: it has yet to come to terms with the implications of Jesus' eschatological beliefs, message, and activity for contemporary faith and ethics. But that is another assignment. Here it is our hope that by asking the right questions—based on the assumptions of the first century rather than our own—we can at least recognize the intention and meaning of these traditions for those who first gave them currency.

2

The Kingdom of God ENTOS HUMŌN ESTIN

Being asked by the Pharisees when the kingdom of God was coming, he answered them, "The Kingdom of God is not coming with signs to be observed; nor will they say, 'Lo, here it is!' or 'There!' for behold, the kingdom of God is in the midst of you" (Luke 17 : 20 f.).

Luke 17 : 21b is one of the celebrated *cruces interpretationis* in New Testament study, particularly in discussions concerning Jesus' conception of the Kingdom of God. It was the favorite proof-text cited by liberal Protestants in support of their contention that the Kingdom of God is (and so also for Jesus was) immanent in human history and society, or, at any rate, in the hearts of men. More recently, it has been construed to mean that Jesus thought that the Kingdom of God was present somehow in his own person. W. G. Kümmel, for instance, hinges upon this verse his thesis that the Kingdom of God was fulfilled in Jesus.[1]

The saying also figures prominently in current discussions of Lucan eschatology. Bent Noack and Hans Conzelmann have seriously proposed as Luke's understanding that the Kingdom of God would come twice. Conzelmann maintains that Luke intended to present a consistent viewpoint with respect to eschatology and the Kingdom of God. The latter has been made manifest in Jesus' person or ministry; it will come again, although only in the remote future.[2] The church, therefore, need not "come to grief" on the problem of the delay of the parousia. Luke 17 : 20 f. expresses Luke's basic apologetic concern: to show that "the Kingdom has appeared in Christ."[3]

A fact generally overlooked in discussions of Lucan eschatology

1. *Promise and Fulfilment,* pp. 35 f.; see also pp. 152–55. Similarly, Hans Conzelmann, *The Theology of St. Luke* (New York, 1960), pp. 121–25.
2. Bent Noack, *Das Gottesreich bei Lukas* (Lund, 1948), p. 47; Conzelmann, *Theology of St. Luke,* pp. 122 ff.
3. Conzelmann, *Theology of St. Luke,* pp. 124 f.

is that all other references to the Kingdom of God in special Lucan traditions or versions contemplate only a future coming of the Kingdom of God—10 : 9, 11; 19 : 11; 21 : 31; and 22 : 18.[4] It would, therefore, be exceptional if 17 : 21b alluded to a present arrival or manifestation of the Kingdom of God.

Much discussion has revolved around the question whether the prepositional phrase *entos humōn* should be translated "within you" or "in the midst of you." Harnack, Dodd, and other liberal and/or Platonizing interpreters usually have favored the former option: "the Kingdom of God is within your hearts." But why should Jesus have told the Pharisees that the Kingdom of God was within *their* hearts (17 : 20)? Various interpreters, beginning with Tertullian, have suggested that Jesus meant that his hearers had it in their power to fulfill God's will: "the Kingdom of God is within your reach."[5] Maurice Goguel reads the verse similarly, but with reference to the future: the possibility of entering the Kingdom will be in you. Most recent interpreters, however, prefer "in your midst" or "amongst you."[6] The decisive question, in that case, becomes whether Jesus meant that the Kingdom was already in the midst of his hearers or that at some future point it would be in their midst. The fact that *estin* ("is") is in the present tense is not decisive, since, as Kümmel notes, "it is usual in Aramaic for the copula to be missing."[7] Furthermore, in Aramaic the present and future forms are indistinguishable. In many of Jesus' sayings about the Kingdom of God or the resurrection the present tense is used when a future time is clearly implied by the context or meaning.[8] Neither *entos humōn* nor *estin* explains the meaning of the

4. Cf. 18 : 1–8; 20 : 34 f.; 21 : 28; 22 : 30; 23 : 42. Conzelmann has to admit that reference to the nearness of the Kingdom in 10 : 9, 11 poses a problem for his thesis, and tries to explain it away as instruction for the future; he resorts to the futile theory that "this generation" (21 : 32) means "humanity in general," and has no explanation for the promise of speedy vindication in 18 : 1–8 (*ibid.*, pp. 114n3, 131).

5. E.g., Colin H. Roberts, "The Kingdom of Heaven (Luke 17 : 21)," *HTR* 41 (1948), 7 f.

6. For further analysis and references concerning *entos humōn* see Bauer, *Lexicon*, p. 269; Kümmel, *Promise and Fulfilment*, pp. 32 ff.; and Noack, *Lukas*, pp. 4 ff. Of course, Jesus himself never said *entos humōn*, but used some Aramaic or Hebrew expression.

7. Kümmel, *Promise and Fulfilment*, p. 34. Cf. Otto, *Kingdom of God*, p. 133. Otto assumes that the implicit copula must have signified the present tense. But this is precisely the point at issue!

8. Mark 9 : 43–48 = Matt. 18 : 8–9; Matt. 18 : 4; Luke 18 : 24 f.; Mark

half verse in question. It is necessary to examine the context in which it appears.

Verb tenses in the adjacent verses are significant. The present tense is used to point to the future coming of the Kingdom of God in the verse containing the Pharisees' question that introduces the pericope, and appears similarly in Jesus' response, which actually is the first part of the sentence that carries through v. 21. Furthermore, the future is clearly intended and the future tense is used in v. 21a and in the description of events with which the saying closes (17 : 22–37).[9]

Another prominent feature of the context, the phrase *ouk . . . meta paratēreseōs* in v. 20b ("not . . . with signs to be observed," RSV), has been variously interpreted. Harnack thought that Jesus meant here to deny that the Kingdom of God would come in any external or visible sense, and to affirm that it comes "inwardly," an interpretation that went rather nicely with his understanding that the Kingdom of God really meant God's rule in the hearts of men. Arnold Meyer, on the other hand, urged the view that *meta paratēreseōs* meant "secretly": "the Kingdom of God does not come so secretly that one must ask, is it here or there. . . ."[10] Usually, however, the term *paratērēsis* and in fact the whole saying have been interpreted in an anti-apocalyptic sense: Jesus intended to deny that it was possible to predict when the Kingdom of God would come by consulting prophecies and deciphering the signs of the times.[11] If the Kingdom had already come, there would be no need at any future time to search for signs of its coming. Is that what Jesus (or Luke) meant? It is not likely. For one thing, Jesus

---

12 : 18–27 and par. It need not be supposed that the Synoptic writers were in error in using the present tense for future time, though the practice might be regarded as Semitic. If they assumed that the resurrection, the coming of the Son of man and Judgment, and entering the Kingdom were all to take place in the future, it would not have been natural for them to make a special point of using the Greek future on every possible occasion. They would not have visualized a need to prove to readers in later centuries that Jesus had expected the Kingdom to come in the near future.

9. Specifically, the future tense appears in vv. 21, 22, 23, 24, 26, 30, 31, 33, 34, 35, (36), and 37.

10. Noack, *Lukas,* p. 7. Meyer, however, regards "suddenly" as counterpart to "secretly." This is not the correct inference.

11. Thus Weiss, *Predigt,* pp. 30 f.; Rudolf Bultmann, *The History of the Synoptic Tradition* (New York, 1963), pp. 125 ff.; Conzelmann, *Theology of St. Luke,* pp. 122 f.

and Luke clearly expected the coming of the Kingdom of God in the future, whether or not they also thought that it was already present or had come previously.

Furthermore, it is not evident that the term *paratērēsis* in v. 20b should be understood to designate a *preliminary* apocalyptic sign at all, at least not the kind of sign that could be used as the basis for calculating the "day and the hour." The preposition *meta* with the genitive conveys the sense of association or accompaniment; where the genitive noun following is impersonal, the usage denotes "the attendant circumstances of something that takes place" or "accompanying phenomena."[12] Despite this fact, Luke 17 : 20 is commonly read by those who see in it an anti-apocalyptical polemic as if it presented an instance of *meta* with the *accusative*: the Kingdom of God is not coming *after* (preliminary) signs. In 17 : 20 f., however, it is not a matter of *preliminary* signs. Rather, Jesus declares, there will be no *accompanying* sign to mark the arrival or imminence of the Kingdom.

The most significant portion of the context has generally been overlooked, namely, Luke 17 : 21a: . . . *oude erousin; idou hōde ē; ekei* (". . . . nor will they say, 'Behold here!' or 'There!'"). It is particularly interesting that this wording, which appears here in connection with the arrival of the Kingdom of God, is repeated nearly verbatim in v. 23, but with explicit reference to the *future* arrival of the days of the Son of man. This parallelism or repetition suggests what is generally evident elsewhere in the synoptic tradition (despite Vielhauer), that Jesus associated the coming of the Kingdom of God with the coming of the Son of man.[13] The latter event, clearly, is thought of as still future (vv. 23 ff.). But while v. 21a reads, ". . . nor will they say, 'Lo, here!' or 'There!,'" v. 23

12. Bauer places *meta paratērēseōs* ("with signs") in this category (*Lexicon*, pp. 510 f.). Other examples of this usage in reference to accompanying eschatological phenomena are Mark 13 : 26 = Matt. 24 : 30 = Luke 21 : 27; and Matt. 24 : 31.

13. Vielhauer argues that Jesus had looked for "the imminent irruption of the Kingdom of God," but that the references to the coming of the Son of man were created by the church in order to replace the Kingdom of God expectation which had failed to materialize. Certainly some of the Son of man sayings reflect the church's problem with the delay of the "parousia." But so do some of the Kingdom of God sayings (see below, pp. 88 ff.). For a careful critique of Vielhauer's thesis, see H. E. Tödt, *The Son of Man in the Synoptic Tradition* (Philadelphia, 1965), pp. 329–47.

reads, "And they *will* say to you, 'Lo, there! Lo, here!'" Why do the prospective bystanders on one occasion claim to have identified or located the Kingdom of God (and/or the days of the Son of man) but on another occasion keep silent? How explain this apparent contradiction? What is the point here? In particular, why, on the one occasion, will they *not* say, "Lo, here!" or "There!"?

The Pharisees, Luke says, have asked Jesus when (*pote*) the Kingdom of God is coming. To this he replies that its coming is not or will not be accompanied by a sign (17 : 20b). Note that they do not ask him about signs. His reply, however, passes over their question concerning "when." Instead, he answers as if they had asked him whether there would be some sign by which the arrival of the final period could be identified, as if he were responding to the second part of the question raised by the disciples in Matt. 24 : 3= Mark 13 : 4=Luke 21 : 7.[14] Interpreters generally have overlooked the fact that Luke 17 : 21a is also a response to this latter kind of question, a question that, to be sure, may be implied in the first: when the time comes, *how will men know that the Kingdom of God is here?* What is said in 17 : 23 f. is obviously in answer to this second point: *when the Son of man comes, there will be no mistake about it.* Thus, those who in the meantime, in the interim before his coming, say, "Lo, there!" or "Here!" should be ignored, "for (*gar*) just as the lightning flashes and lights up the sky from one side to the other, so will the Son of man be in his day." Those guides who will point to some sign or clue in order to prove that the days of the Son of man have come, or will offer to lead Jesus' disciples to a hidden Son of man somewhere, will be in error, therefore, and the disciples should not follow them. This is the meaning of Matt. 24 : 26 f., Luke 21 : 8, and also, perhaps, of the "vultures" saying in Matt. 24 : 28=Luke 17 : 37. Elsewhere, Jesus had stated, against the desire of the Pharisees and "this generation" for a sign (*sēmeion*), that none would be given (Mark 8 : 11 f.). The Markan context does not show whether Jesus (or the Pharisees) had in mind a future sign that would (or would not) accompany the eschatological events, or a sign that might be given in advance. Perhaps the Pharisees sought a sign that would demonstrate Jesus' prophetic authority. Signs and wonders (*sēmeia* and

14. Note the use of *mellō* in Mark 13 : 4 and Luke 21 : 7 : "when all these things are *about to* (or *begin to*) be accomplished." See Bauer, *Lexicon*, p. 502.

terata) are mentioned in Mark 13 : 22 = Matt. 24 : 24; however, these are to identify the presence of false prophets and false Christs. Such might point to signs as evidence of "realized eschatology" (Mark 13 : 21–23 = Matt. 24 : 23–25, 26), but when the real Son of man comes, there will be no need for signs of the times. The evidence will be clearly visible and incontrovertible (Matt. 24 : 27; Mark 13 : 24–27 and par.).

The negative statement . . . *oude erousin; idou hōde ē; ekei* (" . . . nor will they say: lo here, or there") in v. 21a, and the positive declaration . . . *kai erousin humin; idou ekei, idou hōde* (" . . . and they will say to you: lo there, lo here") in v. 23a do not contradict each other. In both instances Jesus is saying exactly the same thing about the Kingdom of God or the Son of man. In the earlier saying, the point is that the Kingdom will not come with an accompanying sign, i.e., in such a way that it will be necessary to look for some way of verifying it in case of doubt. The latter saying warns that in the coming days, before the Kingdom of God has come and while the disciples are passionately longing (*epithumē-sete*) for the coming days of the Son of man,[15] some will claim to have found him (the Son of man) or it (the Kingdom of God); but the disciples must not be misled, for the arrival of the Kingdom of God and Son of man will be so distinctive as to be self-evident and self-authenticating.[16] There will be no doubt about it.

The parallelism extends beyond the anticipated silence and exclamations of the respective future bystanders; in each case, their responses are explained by reference to the character of the coming events, and the explanation is introduced by the conjunction *gar* ("for"). V. 24 explains that the disciples are not to follow those who will mistakenly say "Lo, there!" or "Here!" *for* when the Son of man or the day of the Son of man really comes, it will be just as evident as when the lightning flashes from one side of the sky to the other (cf. Mark 13 : 24–26). Similarly, our *crux interpretationis*, v. 21b, follows v. 21a to explain why, when the Kingdom of God

15. There is no basis for the view that Jesus speaks here of the disciples' future retrospective longing for the good old days when he was still on earth among them, *contra*, e.g., Noack, *Lukas*, p. 44. The days of the Son of man, like the day of the Son of man, are in the future (Luke 17 : 26).

16. It is commonly assumed that just the opposite is true: e.g., E. J. Tinsley, *The Gospel According to Luke* (Cambridge, 1965), p. 166: "It is never that kind of indisputable fact."

really comes (or while it is coming), the bystanders will *not* say, "Lo, here!" or "There!," the reason being (*gar*) that then the Kingdom of God will be visibly and dramatically in their midst. When the Kingdom of God comes, one will neither have to look for any special sign to identify it nor need a guide to find it somewhere.

The reason it is pointless to look for signs is not that the coming of the Kingdom of God and the Son of man will be invisible, but that, on the contrary, it will be universally and unmistakably visible, "as the lightning flashes and lights up the sky from one side to the other." That is why, *then* the bystanders will *not* say, "Lo, here!" or "There!" And that is also why those who *in the meantime* say "Lo, there!" or "Here!" are to be ignored.

It could be argued that the parallelism between 17 : 20 f. and 17 : 23 f. represents only Luke's understanding of the matter, that these verses were not part of an original pericope, and that Luke has woven them together (or even created some of them) in accordance with his own ideas and literary style.[17] In that case, however, one would still have to conclude that in 17 : 21b Luke understands Jesus to have meant that the coming of the Kingdom of God would be a future, obvious, and all-encompassing event, for this is exactly the point which the parallelism expresses. Since the only source for the half verse in question is Luke's Gospel, its evident meaning to this evangelist is the only clue we have to its interpretation. All of the sayings in Luke 17:20–18:8 have to do with the coming of the Kingdom of God and the Son of man, and with the responses men will or should make in the interim and at the time the Kingdom and Son of man are revealed. Throughout this section, it is clear that these decisive events are to take place in the future, though—contrary to Conzelmann—not necessarily in the remote future.[18] Elsewhere also, as has been mentioned, the peculiarly Lu-

17. Bultmann considers Luke 17 : 23 f. a variant of 17 : 20 f., but mistakenly supposes that the saying refers to the *sudden* coming of the Kingdom, against those who wished to calculate the time of its arrival (*History of the Synoptic Tradition*, pp. 121 f., 125). There is nothing about suddenness or calculating in either version, however. To be sure, lightning flashes suddenly. But the alternative to "here" or "there" is not *suddenly*, but *everywhere*: "from one side to the other." When the Kingdom of God or the days of the Son of man arrive, there will be no doubt about it. Luke's belief that the new era would be universally recognizable appears also in his paraphrase of Isa. 40 : 5: "And all flesh shall see the salvation of God" (3 : 6).

18. See C. E. B. Cranfield, "The Parable of the Unjust Judge and the Eschatology of Luke–Acts," *SJT* 16 (1963), 298.

can material speaks only of a future coming of the Kingdom of God. It may be that Luke understood that certain *eschatological* events had taken place already in or with the ministry of Jesus: for example, the coming of Elijah (Luke 1 : 16 f., 76) or the preaching of the time of salvation (Luke 4 : 17 ff.). There is, however, no reason to suppose that Luke thought that the *Kingdom of God* has come or appeared in or with Jesus and his ministry. Lucan eschatology is unequivocally futuristic, so far as the Kingdom of God is concerned.

What Jesus meant by the saying in Luke 17 : 20 f., if it is properly attributable to him, cannot be determined as a matter of certainty. If Luke's presentation of it is correct, however, it does not support the view that Jesus considered the Kingdom of God to be present in his own person, or, for that matter, present at all. On the contrary, these verses point to its appearance dramatically and unmistakably in the future. When Luke 17 : 21b is taken in its context, the meaning emerges clearly enough: when the Kingdom of God comes, everyone will know it; there will be no need for authenticating clues or signs. Such also was the OT expectation— "the glory of the Lord shall be revealed, and all flesh shall see it together" (Isa. 40 : 5).

3

The Kingdom of God EPHTHASEN EPH' HUMAS

But if it is by the Spirit of God that I cast out demons, then the Kingdom of God has come upon you (Matt. 12 : 28 = Luke 11 : 20).

THIS SENTENCE implies a definite relationship between exorcism of demons and the coming of the Kingdom of God. The question is: What kind of relationship?

It is usually supposed that Jesus is able to cast out demons because the Kingdom of God, or "its power," is now present and operative. His power over the demons should be seen by the Pharisees as a sign that the Kingdom of God has already come. There is another possibility, however: Jesus' campaign against the demons is preliminary and preparatory to the coming of the Kingdom of God. From the fact that Jesus is defeating the demons, the Pharisees should recognize that the final victory is near, that the Kingdom of God will soon be established on earth.

Before attempting to resolve this question, a few literary features of the pericope should be observed. The saying in question, together with the preceding verse (Matt. 12 : 27=Luke 11 : 19), do not appear in Mark. They are placed by both Matthew and Luke, appropriately, in the so-called Beelzebul controversy. It is not clear who Jesus' accusers were: in Mark (3:22) they are scribes from Jerusalem; in Matthew they are "the Pharisees" (12 : 24); and in Luke they are simply some of "the people" (11 : 14 f.). In any case they are skeptics who accuse Jesus of casting out demons by (the power or authority of) Beelzebul. In Mark, Jesus responds by suggesting that Satan would be foolish to lay waste to his own kingdom or house (3 : 23–26 and par.), and that before one can enter a strong man's house to plunder, he must first bind the strong man (3:27 and par.). The "Q" saying adds the *ad hominem* argument "If I cast out demons by Beelzebul, by whom do your associates do so?" followed by the adversative *ei de* ("but if") which introduces the possibility his accusers have overlooked or denied— that it is by the power (finger or Spirit) of God that Jesus commands the demons. Instead of working by the power of "the prince of demons," "an unclean spirit" (Mark 3 : 30), Jesus declares that he works by the power of the Holy Spirit (Mark 3 : 29 and par.), the Spirit of God.[1]

It should be noted that the controversy between Jesus and his opponents does not center upon the question whether the Kingdom of God was present or future. The issue is whether Jesus' exorcisms are authorized by Beelzebul, the prince of demons, or by the Spirit of God. But when asserting that the latter was the case, Jesus adds, as a warning to his opponents, "then" or "in this case" (*ara*) the Kingdom of God *ephthasen eph' humas* ("has come upon you"). It is not likely that he was telling them that the Kingdom of God was "within" them, "in their hearts," any more here than in Luke 17 : 20 f.[2] The saying appears rather as a solemn promise or threat, like the terrible saying in Mark 3 : 29 and par. about those who commit blasphemy against the Holy Spirit.

This sense of threatening catastrophe is precisely the meaning Kenneth Clark has found *phthanein* to have in various early Jewish writings—e.g., Judges 20 : 42 (LXX)—"to press close." The idea is that of "pursuit and imminent contact."[3] Jesus' exact attitude toward the scribes and Pharisees cannot be stated with certainty. In Mark, as J. M. Robinson has pointed out, Jesus' "debates" with his opponents closely parallel the exorcisms: in both cases, Mark (if not Jesus) visualizes a cosmic struggle between Satan's demons and supporters (including the Jewish authorities), and Jesus and his followers who are faithful to God.[4] Something of the same evaluation, specifically, of the scribes and Pharisees, appears in Matthew, where they are characterized as a "child of Gehenna," "serpents," "brood of vipers" destined to condemnation in Gehenna (23 : 15, 33). The thrust of Matt. 12 : 28 seems to be that the defeat

1. It is likely that "Spirit of God" (= Holy Spirit, cf. "unclean spirit") is the earlier reading. See Eduard Schweizer et al., *Spirit of God* (London, 1960), pp. 37 ff.

2. See above, Chapter 2.

3. Kenneth W. Clark, "Realized Eschatology," *JBL* 59 (1940), 377.

4. *The Problem of History in Mark*, SBT no. 21 (London, 1957), pp. 43–51.

of the demons and the coming of the kingdom is bad news for the Pharisees, Jesus' accusers. This is certainly the sense of Matt. 12 : 31–32: Those who blaspheme "against the Holy Spirit will not be forgiven, either in *this age* or in *the age to come*."[5]

It is clear from this reference to the "two ages" that Matthew understood that Jesus and his contemporaries were still living in "this age." In that case, the Kingdom of God had not yet come.[6] Several references to the Kingdom appear in the special Lukan material ("L"). In all of them where time is indicated, it is evident that Luke understood Jesus to expect the arrival of the Kingdom at some time in the future.[7] It is possible that 11 : 20 is an exception to Luke's understanding of the matter; but it seems more probable that he, like Matthew, regarded this saying as referring to the future, if imminent, arrival of the Kingdom. In the same chapter, Luke refers to the future judgment in store for "this generation" (11 : 30–32, 50 f.).

It will be objected, however, that this saying, and perhaps others also, mean the proleptic actualization of the Kingdom,[8] or at least the presence and effective operation of the powers of the inbreaking Kingdom of God.[9] In fact, a great many categories have been invented in order to describe the situation of the Kingdom of God during Jesus' ministry: it was *dawning* or *breaking in*; the *shift of aeons* was taking place; it was already present *proleptically*; its *powers* were operative in Jesus' exorcisms. It should be noted that none of these italicized expressions, though often repeated in the secondary literature, is to be found in the synoptic tradition.[10] In the passage in question, it is not the "powers of the Kingdom of God" that are at work; it is not even the Kingdom of God that is described as operative. Instead, it is

5. Italics added. It is likely that Jesus, like Matthew, thought in terms of the two ages, rather than the abstract category of eternity. See my article "Not the Season for Figs," *JBL* 87 (1968), 397 f. The Christian liturgical "world without end" distorts the sense of *eis ton aiōna*: "until the Age to come," or "in the Age to come."

6. The "Kingdom of God" and the "Age to Come" are synonomous.

7. See above, Chapter 2, pp. 22 f.

8. Reginald H. Fuller, *The Foundations of New Testament Christology* (New York, 1965), p. 105.

9. Otto, *Kingdom of God*, p. 102n1; James M. Robinson, *A New Quest of the Historical Jesus*, SBT no. 25 (London, 1959), pp. 109 f.

10. The "powers" mentioned in Mark 6 : 14 are supernatural and, possibly, eschatological, but are not designated powers of the Kingdom of God.

the "Spirit" (or "finger") of God, thus, if one insists upon another
term, the power of God himself which is to be seen in the exorcisms (cf. Acts 10 : 38). The presence of the power of God or his
Spirit, however, is not the same as the presence of the Kingdom of
God.[11]

But what relation is there between the Spirit of God active in
exorcising demons, and the coming of the Kingdom of God?
Howard Kee has shown that the verb *gāʿár* (*epitiman*, "to rebuke") in the OT, Qumran, and synoptic literatures has the sense
not simply of exorcism, but also involves the subjugation of "the
evil spirits in order that God's dominion may become a reality."[12]
Study of Matt. 12 : 28 = Luke 11 : 20 has, to date, overlooked the
eschatological significance of exorcism: specifically, the point that
the overcoming of the demons (and thus of Satan's power) contributes to Satan's defeat and thereby prepares the way for the
coming of the Kingdom of God. Furthermore, those liberated from
the demons are prepared for the possibility of entering the Kingdom of God. Perhaps this is the meaning of baptism "with the
Holy Spirit" (Mark 1 : 8 and par.), at least as Mark understood it.

When the Kingdom of God comes, Satan and his demons will
no longer have place on earth. When the Kingdom of God comes,
it will mean that God rules the earth, no longer Satan (cf. Luke
4 : 5 f.). Until then, the Evil One continues to be a source of peril
to earth's inhabitants.[13] However, the victories over Satan's demons
gained by Jesus (and his disciples) mean that Satan's doom is
certain. Such, we suggest, is also the sense of Mark 3 : 27, Luke
10 : 17 f., and the rather more enigmatic Matt. 11 : 12.[14] The connection between exorcism and the Kingdom of God, then, is that
the former prepares for the coming of the latter.

That the exorcistic work of Jesus and his disciples is preliminary
to the coming of the Kingdom of God is substantiated elsewhere in
the synoptic tradition. Generally this is to be seen in the fact that
Jesus performs exorcisms throughout his ministry (at any rate in
the first reported portions of it [Mark 1–7, 9]), while maintaining

11. Contrary to a widespread tendency to equate the two: e.g., O. Betz,
"Jesu Heiliger Krieg," *NT* 2 (1958), 126 ff.; Schweizer, *Spirit of God*, pp.
26 f.
12. "The Terminology of Mark's Exorcism Stories," *NTS* 14 (1968), 232–
46, esp. 235, 239, 243.
13. Cf. Matt. 6 : 10, 13; Mark 4 : 15 =Matt. 13 : 19b.
14. See below, Chapters 4–6.

consistently that the Kingdom and/or parousia are in the future.[15] More specifically, we find that Jesus sent out his followers to preach repentance and the nearness of the Kingdom and at the same time —as part of the same mission—to cast out demons and heal the sick.[16] Their proclamation about the Kingdom as reported in Matt. 10 : 7 and Luke 10 : 9, 11 leaves no doubt about its futurity: *ēngiken hē basileia tōn ouranōn* ("the Kingdom of heaven has come near"). Professor Clark has shown that *engizein* cannot have meant simply "has come."[17] In these passages it must mean that the Kingdom has come near or close, or that it soon will come. Such evidently was Matthew's understanding (10 : 23). If elsewhere Jesus' exorcisms and those wrought by his disciples were thought of as preliminary to the coming of the Kingdom, there seems to be no reason why the exorcisms in Matt. 12 : 28 = Luke 11 : 20 should be thought to presuppose its presence.

Finally, however, it might be urged that Jesus thought the Kingdom present in his (and his disciples') operations against the opposing Kingdom of Satan, as the government of a country is represented by its troops that clash upon the field with those of an enemy country. This has been proposed by Rudolf Otto and Floyd Filson, and more recently suggested by Otto Betz and Howard Kee. It is certainly possible that such an understanding is implicit in Matt. 11 : 12. In that case, one could speak of the Kingdom of God as gaining ground against the Kingdom of Satan. The former Kingdom is present as a "beachhold," invading the Kingdom of Satan.[18]

Again, however, it must be pointed out that though *we* may speak in these terms, they have little basis in the synoptic evidence. Here there is no talk of the Kingdom "gaining ground" or "invading" the realm of Satan, any more than there is of its "consummation" or "completion" at a later stage. One is inclined to agree with J. Weiss that for Jesus and the disciples, the Kingdom was either here or not yet here.[19]

Even if one were to speak of its presence in the struggle of Jesus

---

15. Mark 1 : 15; 9 : 1; 10 : 40; 13 : 30 f.; 14 : 25, 62; and par.
16. Mark 6 : 7–13 (cf. 3 : 14 f.); Matt. 9:35–10:23; Luke 9 : 1–6, 10 : 1–12.
17. Clark, "Realized Eschatology," pp. 367–71.
18. Thus G. B. Caird, *The Gospel of St. Luke* (Harmondsworth, Eng., 1963), p. 154.
19. *Predigt*, p. 18.

and his followers against the demons (and Jewish authorities?), this kind of cosmic, dualistic "presence" would be no less "mythological" or alien to our viewpoint than is his otherwise evident understanding that the Kingdom would come in the future.[20] And it would still be true that in the great majority of other instances— if not all of them!—Jesus is represented as looking for the coming of the Kingdom of God only in the future.

It seems more likely, however, that the statement "the Kingdom of God *ephthasen eph' humas*" is simply parallel in meaning to the sayings that appear elsewhere (Mark 1 : 15 = Matt. 4 : 17; Matt. 10 : 7 = Luke 10 : 9; Luke 10 : 11) which announce the nearness of the expected Kingdom of God.

20. See *ibid.*, pp. 18–23. What matters, of course, is what we find, not what we wish to find. The point here is that dogmatic concern to find a Jesus congenial to modern thought or theology can derive little comfort from a Kingdom of God present in the form of cosmic warfare.

4

The Kingdom of God BIAZETAI

From the days of John the Baptist until now, the Kingdom of Heaven has suffered violence, and men of violence have taken it by force (RSV, Matt. 11 : 12; cf. Luke 16 : 16).

IT IS PROBABLE that the Lukan recension of this "Q" saying is secondary. The Matthean is clearly the more "difficult." Luke seems to have reworked it with a view to making it intelligible and, possibly, less offensive: the Kingdom of God is subject to preaching, but not violence. Men do not "seize it by force" (*harpazousin autēn*) as in Matthew, but "press into it" (*eis autēn biazetai*) (cf. Matt. 7 : 13 f. = Luke 13 : 23 f.). Braumann suggests that the meaning of the saying may have been no longer understood by the ancient collector of "Q" himself.[1] In any case, few would argue with Schniewind's observation that "the explication of Matthew 11 : 12 belongs to the most difficult questions of gospel interpretation."[2]

Therefore it is not surprising that the saying has given rise to a number of diverse (and in some cases fantastic) interpretations. The thought of men of violence seizing the Kingdom has, naturally, suggested political-military revolution, after the fashion of Theudas and Judas (Acts 5 : 36 f.) or the Zealots.[3] J. Weiss proposed that Jesus meant to rebuke the Baptist for having aroused such a movement.[4] Schweitzer, on the other hand, proposed that Jesus and his followers were the "men of violence" who would compel the Kingdom to come through the repentance awakened by their preach-

1. George Braumann, "Dem Himmelreich Wird Gewalt Angetan," *ZNW* 52 (1961), 106.
2. Julius Schniewind, *Das Evangelium nach Matthäus* (Göttingen, 1950), p. 144.
3. F. W. Green, *The Gospel according to Saint Matthew* (Oxford, 1936), p. 175.
4. *Predigt*, pp. 15 f., 24 f. Also, Billerbeck, i, 598 f.

ing.[5] Schniewind turns this around and says that it was the Pharisees who had, impiously, talked about "compelling the end" by repentance and obedience to the law. Against them, Schniewind says,
Jesus declared that beginning with John, "the rule of God has
broken in," the "new age" has begun, and the sentence of judgment
stands against all human deeds, especially against pharisaic piety.[6]
One suspects some Lutheran piety and polemics in this exegesis.

Suzanne de Dietrich turns Weiss' suggestion around: Jesus com-
mends the Baptist for winning the Kingdom "by main force, by
asceticism and heroic obedience (v. 12)."[7] Similarly, Rudolf Otto
(following more nearly the sense of Luke 16 : 16) urges that Jesus
meant his hearers to know that "only by summoning all one's power,
and with the most strenuous determination, does one press into
it."[8]

Braumann, on the other hand, finds the decisive parallel in
Phil. 2 : 6. Our saying originated in the early Church to counter
the reproach of those who asserted that "Christ Jesus wanted to
grasp God-likeness for himself." The *biastai* ("men of violence"),
on this theory, stand for the non-Christian world which persecutes
(*biazetai*) the Church.[9]

In dealing with this verse, the following two questions are central: (1) Has the Kingdom of God been "suffering violence" (*biazetai*, passive), *or* has it been "coming violently" (*biazetai*,
middle)? (2) Are the *biastai* (those who are "strong" or "violent"
and "have been snatching it away" or "carrying it away by force,"
harpazousin) the demons or forces of evil, including, perhaps the
Evil One, Satan, himself, *or* are they those who are on the side of
God and His Kingdom, namely Jesus and his disciples? The two
questions are closely related: if the Kingdom of God has been
suffering violence, it probably was thought of as resulting from the
activities of Satan and his forces. On the other hand, if the Kingdom has been coming violently, or by force, this would more likely
be through the activities of Jesus and his disciples.

Quite possibly, Jesus considered that the time of tribulation had

5. *Mystery*, pp. 64 f. Billerbeck lists several rabbinical sayings indicative
of this view (1, 599 ff.).
6. *Matthäus*, pp. 144 f.
7. *The Gospel According to Matthew* (Richmond, 1961), p. 70.
8. *Kingdom of God*, p. 111.
9. "Himmelreich," pp. 107 ff.

already begun, at least for John, in the form of the latter's imprison-ment and death. The phrase "from the days of John the Baptist" intimates that the Baptist's days were now over.[10] Luke's version of the saying (Luke 16 : 16) appears in a different context (not in Luke 7 : 18–35 where one might expect it), well after his ac-count of John's execution by Herod (Luke 9 : 7–9).

The verb *harpazein* ("to snatch away"), which is used in Matt. 11 : 12 to describe the activities of the *biastai*, occurs only two other times in the synoptic gospels, both in Matthew, and in both of these places describes the struggle going on between Jesus, on behalf of the Kingdom of God, and the Evil One and his forces (Matt. 12 : 29, 13 : 19). A similar idea is found in Jesus' warning about "ravenous wolves" (*lukoi harpages*) in Matt. 7 : 15, where the cognate adjective appears, suggesting that these are satanic and not simply misguided prophets.[11]

In Matt. 12 : 29, Jesus raises the question "How can one enter a strong man's house and plunder (*harpasai*) his goods, unless he first binds the strong man? Then indeed he may plunder (*diarpa-sei*)[12] his house." The context, both here and in the Markan parallel (3 : 27), makes it fairly clear that here the "strong man" (*ho is-churos*) is Satan.[13] Are Satan and his forces the "strong men" (*bias-tai*) who are plundering or taking the Kingdom of God by force (*harpazousin*) in Matt. 11 : 12? Of course, there is no way of know-ing what Aramaic terms Jesus may have used, and the Greek noun *biastēs* in Matt. 11 : 12 is *hapax*. Its cognate, *biaios*, is used only once in the NT, in Acts 2 : 2, but occurs frequently in the LXX along with other translations of *'az* ("strong," "violent," etc.) whose nominal cognate, *'oz* ("strength," "violence"), is rendered in the LXX, along with other nouns, by *ischus*, the Greek nominal cognate of *ischuros*. In other words, Jesus could have used the same word for Satan, the "strong man" of Matt. 12 : 29, that he used in 11 : 12, or, for that matter, different words which nevertheless mean the same thing in both cases, namely, Satan and his demons.

10. So also Alan H. M'Neile, *The Gospel According to St. Matthew* (Lon-don, 1915), p. 155.

11. Cf. Matt. 10 : 16=Luke 10 : 3, and John 10 : 12 where the wolf "snatches" (*harpazei*) the sheep.

12. The cognate *diarpazein* also appears twice in the Markan parallel (Mark 3 : 27), but nowhere else in the NT. Both *harpazein* and *diarpazein* are used in the LXX for *gāzal*, "to pull, seize, rob, plunder."

13. See below, however, Chapter 5.

In any case, it is "the Evil One" (*ho poneros*)[14] who comes and "snatches away" or "takes by force" (*harpazei*) the word of the Kingdom according to Matt. 13 : 19. John 10 : 12 may preserve a parallel or interpretation of this same saying: there the wolf snatches and scatters the sheep (cf. John 10 : 28, 29). Similarly, *ho poneros* is directly associated with, and probably considered responsible for, the *peirasmos*, the tribulation expected in the time before the coming of God's Kingdom (Matt. 6 : 13). Is the tribulation in part, then, Satan's last effort to snatch away those otherwise destined for the Kingdom of God?

In this connection, it is interesting to notice Bonner's observation that in Greek and Hebraic exorcisms of the period the exorcised demon typically marks his departure by an act of physical violence, as in Mark 1 : 26, 5 : 13, and 9 : 26.[15] At all events, the demons were thought to cause illness and, occasionally, violent harm to those they possessed: e.g., Mark 5 : 3 ff.; 9 : 18, 20, 22. Sickness, misery, and destruction were characteristic of life in the world ruled by Satan and his demons. Similarly for the Qumran community, the present was seen as the time of Belial's rule and affliction of the pious.[16]

The picture presented in this evidence shows Satan and his demons engaged in a struggle to maintain the rule or authority which they hold over the world and men (cf. Luke 4 : 5 f.), by affliction and tribulation seeking to prevent men from keeping faith in God,[17] and thereby render them unfit for participation in God's Kingdom. Moreover, so long as Satan and the demons rule on earth, God's Kingdom is not yet established here. God's rule over the earth has been interrupted. He is no longer King over all the earth, at least not as the apocalyptic outlook understands the situation.[18] Satan still has to be reckoned with on earth.

14. In Mark 4 : 15, *ho satanas*, Satan.

15. Campbell Bonner, "The Technique of Exorcism," *HTR* 36 (1943), 47–49.

16. Betz, "Heiliger Krieg," p. 117. Betz notes that in IQH 2 : 20–29, the "strong" or "violent men" are members of the Belial community. On the relation between demons and disease in Rabbinic thought, see Billerbeck iv, pt. 1, 524 ff.

17. Cf. Matt. 6 : 13; Mark 13 : 19 f., 14 : 37 f.; Luke 22 : 31 f.; Job 1–2; and *Testament of Daniel* 6 : 1–4.

18. E.g., Dan. 2, 7–12; Zech. 14 : 9; *Jubilees* 10 : 8; Rev.; and IQM. See Paul Volz, *Die Eschatologie der judischen Gemeinde* (Tübingen, 1934), pp. 68–89; and Walter Grundmann, *Der Begriff der Kraft in der neutestamentlichen Gedankenwelt* (Stuttgart, 1932), pp. 47 ff.

On the other hand, it may be that Jesus meant that he and his disciples were the "strong men" of Matt. 11 : 12, those who "take the Kingdom of God by force." Jesus and his followers are engaged in a campaign against Satan's demons. In Matt. 12 : 29 it is, implicitly, Jesus who will enter the "strong man's" house to plunder (*harpasei*) his goods.[19] One does not bind a strong man without violence or force! Jesus does not shrink from describing the coming of the Son of man as being like the coming of a thief in the night.[20] One should not be shocked if he applied the image of the robber to himself when speaking of his activities against the household of Satan. He sees the victories of the disciples over the demons as basis for his conviction, experienced, perhaps, as a vision, that Satan either had fallen or would fall from the heavens (Luke 10 : 17 f.), and as confirmation of the authority (*exousia*) which he had given them over the power (*dunamis*) of the Enemy.

The Baptist had described the one coming after himself who would baptize with the Holy Spirit as *ho ischuroteros mou* ("the one who is stronger than me").[21] In Luke 11 : 22 Jesus is described as "one stronger (*ischuroteros*) than" the "strong man." Here Jesus is thought of as doing violence to the kingdom of Satan, much as in their mission(s) throughout Israel his disciples also exercise the power (*dunamis, exousia*) which he has given them over the demons,[22] while proclaiming the need for repentance and the nearness of the Kingdom of God. Elsewhere Luke speaks of Jesus' healing those afflicted by the devil through the efficacy of the Holy Spirit and power (*dunamis*) with which God had anointed him (Acts 10 : 38). Jesus was the only one strong enough (*ischuen*) to subdue the demoniac whom no one else could bind (*dēsai*) (Mark 5 : 3 f.).

On the basis of his review of Qumran writings, Betz proposes that several of Jesus' sayings, including Matt. 11 : 12, can best be accounted for if he is pictured as a warrior on behalf of the King-

---

19. If the "strong man" represents the demon(s), the "goods" would be the men delivered from the demons, rather than the demons themselves; but the meaning would be essentially the same. Jesus would be "plundering" men— snatching them away from Satan's power—and by freeing them from the demons, preparing them for participation in the Kingdom of God. Those who were still possessed by Satan's demons would not, of course, be in any position to enter the Kingdom of God.

20. Matt. 24 : 43 f. = Luke 12 : 39 f. Cf. I Thess. 5 : 2.

21. Mark 1 : 7 and par.

22. E.g., Mark 6 : 7–14; Matt. 10 : 1 ff.; Luke 9 : 1–6, 10 : 1–20.

dom of God, using the power of God's Spirit in carrying on the "holy war" against the demons and earthly opponents of God's people.[23] Something of the sort is certainly intimated in Matt. 12 : 28 = Luke 11 : 20 and Mark 3 : 27. The demons perceive that Jesus' mission is to destroy them (Mark 1 : 24); and conversely, the Pharisees, who in Mark are part of the Satanic opposition to Jesus,[24] work at their plan to destroy him (Mark 3 : 6). Howard Kee, who also grounds his study upon the Dead Sea Scrolls, finds that exorcism—"rebuking" (gā'ár) the evil spirits—had as its goal their subjugation "in order that the Rule of God might be established."[25] Kee proposes that Jesus' mission was conceived similarly by Mark: In accordance with his cosmic plan, God "was regaining control over an estranged and hostile creation, which was under subjection to the powers of Satan. Jesus' exorcisms are depicted in the oldest layers of the gospel tradition as contributing to the fulfillment of that eschatological goal."[26]

Whether one reads *biazetai* in the middle or passive, and understands *hoi biastai* to designate Satan and his demons or Jesus and his disciples, it is clear that a significant interim or final period is here indicated: the period since John the Baptist, which probably means since his death, but prior to the establishment of the Kingdom of God on earth. This period "between the times" was inaugurated by the appearance of the Baptist, whom Jesus identified as Elijah, the preacher of repentance prior to the parousia and judgment; it would end with the conclusion of the final sufferings or tribulation.[27]

Whether the Kingdom of God has been coming violently or suffering violence, the meaning is approximately the same: the struggle for dominion over the earth has started. In war, both sides "suffer violence," and the end, victory, "comes with violence." Perhaps the saying presupposes the beginning of the period of final tribulation (*ho peirasmos*) which is at once the final effort

23. "Heiliger Krieg," pp. 125–28.

24. Thus Robinson, *Problem of History in Mark*, pp. 43–51, and Betz, "Heiliger Krieg," p. 128.

25. "Terminology," p. 235. Kee finds this concept in several of the Qumran writings, e.g., IQGA, IQM, 4QMª.

26. "Terminology," p. 246.

27. Matt. 11 : 14, and below, Chapter 7; Mark 13 : 19–27; cf. Dan. 7 : 9–22, 8 : 18–25.

of the forces of Satan to crush the faithful and prevent God's Kingdom from coming, and at the same time, since this effort is doomed,
the birth pangs of the messianic age (*hē ōdin*).[28] In any case, Jesus
and his disciples have engaged the forces of the enemy. They must
be prepared for tribulation and temptation (Mark 13 : 8 ff., 14 :
38), but they can endure and even conquer, for through the power
of the Spirit of God which is the source of their authority or power
over the demons, they can actually overpower them and thus be
assured of and contribute to the ultimate defeat of Satan and the
victory of God's Kingdom on earth.

28. The evangelists, however, seem to have expected the "woes" or "birth
pangs" to begin in the future, or perhaps thought these had begun with the destruction of Jerusalem: Mark 13 : 8 and par. See also Billerbeck, i, 950.

5

Binding and Plundering the Strong Man and His House

But no one can enter a strong man's house and plunder his goods, unless he first binds the strong man; then indeed he may plunder his house (Mark 3 : 27).

THIS SAYING appears in virtually the same form in Matt. 12 : 29, except that there it is in the form of a question, following the pattern of 12 : 27, and the verb *harpazein* ("to snatch away") is used in 29a instead of the cognate *diarpazein* ("to plunder"). Both verbs suggest conflict between Satan and God's people (cf. Matt. 11 : 12, 13 : 19). The Lukan version, however, is probably secondary.[1]

The Markan-Matthean saying probably is based upon the language of Isaiah 49 : 24 f. and/or *Psalms of Solomon* 5 : 4. In later times, the imagery was developed in connection with the thought that after his death Jesus descended into Hades and liberated those held captive there by Satan.[2] Here, however, the reference is clearly to Jesus' activity against Satan or the demons during his earthly ministry. It is, to some extent, recognized that Mark pictures Jesus' ministry as a continuous struggle against the forces of Satan.[3] The immediate context in Mark is the "Beelzebul controversy" which follows directly after Mark's account of Jesus' healing many who had been oppressed by "unclean spirits" (3 : 7–12), and his commissioning of the twelve, to cast out demons and preach (3 : 13–19). In Mark, the "Twelve" have as their dual assignment preaching (repentance) *and* casting out demons by the authority

1. Luke 11 : 21 f. reflects the language of Isa. 53 : 12 LXX, and may manifest Luke's characteristic concern that the wealth of the rich be shared with the poor: thus S. Legasse, " 'L'Homme fort' de Luc 11 : 21–22," NT 5 (1962), 6–9.
2. Eph. 4 : 8–10; I Peter 3 : 18–20; Marcion.
3. This has been ably demonstrated in Robinson, *Problem of History in Mark*.

43

given them by Jesus (6 : 7–13). Both activities represent an extension of Jesus' own ministry (1 : 39), and were probably understood in the expression "fishers of men" (1 : 17). Mark calls attention to the authority (*exousia*) with which Jesus both taught and commanded the demons (1 : 22, 27). Elsewhere in the synoptics also we read of Jesus' granting authority to his followers, both explicitly and implicitly, to cast out demons.[4]

The "controversy" itself focuses upon this question: By whose authority does Jesus cast out demons? The "scribes" do not question Jesus' ability to control the evil spirits, but they charge that he works by the authority of Beelzebul or "the prince of demons."[5] Jesus' answer, both in Mark 3 : 28–30 and Matt. 12 : 28, is that his authority or power is that of the Spirit of God or Holy Spirit, not that of an unclean or unholy spirit. Luke also suggests that Jesus' exorcisms were empowered by the Holy Spirit in Peter's "speech" in Acts 10 : 38, even though Luke usually associates the Holy Spirit only with prophecy and speaking in tongues.

The idea that the King or Messiah would have the power of the Spirit of God is firmly rooted in the OT.[6] It is not certain, however, that Jesus and his contemporaries would have necessarily regarded these Spirit-authorized exorcisms as a *messianic* activity. As Grundmann notes, it could have been thought of as *prophetic* power, as in Luke 24 : 19 and 1 : 17. The latter, looking to the future role of the Baptist, speaks of "the Spirit and the power of Elijah." Jesus' "mighty works" suggest, at least to some, that *he* is Elijah (Matt. 11 : 1 ff.; Mark 6 : 15, 8 : 28). In some of the Jewish literature, however, it was expected that the Son of Man or Messiah-priest would do battle with the demons in order to overcome Satan's rule on earth, thereby preparing for the coming of the Kingdom of God.[7] If we could be certain that working by the

4. Luke 9 : 1 = Matt. 10 : 1; Luke 10 : 19; 10 : 22a = Matt. 11 : 27a; Matt. 16 : 19, 18 : 18, 28 : 18.

5. It is not certain that Beelzebul = Satan. The scribes may have made two charges: that Jesus is possessed by the evil spirit named Beelzebul (cf. v. 30), and that he works by authority of the prince of demons, namely, Satan. The names Belial (Beliar) and Mastema also appear in the intertestamental literature. "The devil," "the Evil One," and Satan are used interchangeably in the gospels.

6. I Sam. 11 : 6, 16 : 13; Isa. 11 : 2; *Psalms of Solomon* 17 : 37 f. See also Grundmann, *Begriff*, pp. 55 ff.

7. See Volz, *Eschatologie*, pp. 188 ff.; Billerbeck, IV, pt. 1, 502 ff. See esp.

power of the Spirit were an exclusively messianic prerogative, we could regard Jesus' exorcistic work as a clue to his "messianic self-consciousness." Probably this is how Mark viewed the matter, for, as he describes it, Jesus' conflict with Satan and the demons begins dramatically with the descent of the Spirit upon him at his baptism, and the voice from heaven (Mark 1 : 11) pronounces the decisive phrase from the OT messianic coronation psalm, 2 : 7. But since the Spirit was to be poured out on "all flesh" in the days before the final deliverance (Joel 2 : 28 ff.), and since, especially in Luke, the Spirit is manifested in many persons, we cannot conclude definitely that Jesus regarded his Spirit-authorized activity against the demons as messianic, i.e., a function of the Messiah.

The Christological question is not at issue in the pericope, however. Here, simply, the scribes have accused Jesus of working *for* Satan. Whatever it may mean more precisely, it is clear that the intention of 3 : 27 is to deny this charge by stating that Jesus is working *against* Satan.

The exact meaning of the saying, however, is elusive. Frequently the meaning is assumed to be that Jesus has already bound Satan, having defeated him in the wilderness (Mark 1 : 13).[8] The previous defeat of Satan now makes it possible for Jesus to "plunder" Satan's household, i.e., destroy the demons and liberate their victims. Jesus' vision of Satan's "fall from heaven" (Luke 10 : 18) is sometimes cited in support of this theory. As will be seen, however, Luke 10 : 18 probably has a different meaning.[9] Mark 1 : 13 says nothing about Jesus' having "defeated" Satan: here he only withstood the "temptation." Furthermore, in 3 : 27 Jesus seems to be speaking of the meaning of his present activity. How could he have expected the scribes to know what had happened in "the wilderness"? Moreover, in the next chapter, Mark reports that

---

T. Zebulon 9 : 8; *T. Daniel* 5 : 10; *T. Levi* 18 : 9 ff.; cf. Zech. 3–6. *T. Zeb.* 9 : 8 and *T. Dan.* 5 : 11, however, contain echoes of Mal. 4 : 2, 6, respectively, and may therefore point to Elijah rather than a messianic figure. Some references to the Messiah in the *Testament of the Twelve* may be Christian interpolations.

8. So, for instance, Paul S. Minear, *Mark* (Richmond, 1962), p. 66; Walter Grundmann, *Das Evangelium nach Markus,* 3rd ed. (Berlin, 1965), p. 35, who sees Jesus' "victory" there as fulfilling the work of the messianic high priest of *T. Levi* 18. Another proposal is that *God* on some previous occasion had defeated Satan: thus Otto, *Kingdom of God,* pp. 103 f.

9. See below, Chapter 6.

Jesus spoke of the continuing menace Satan presents (4 : 13 f.). J. M. Robinson seems to be correct in stating that Mark regards all of the exorcisms "in terms of the cosmic struggle between the Spirit and Satan begun in the temptation."[10] In this case, Jesus' activity would not presuppose that Satan had already been defeated or "bound."

We cannot be absolutely sure, in fact, that the "strong man" in v. 27 is Satan. The designation *ho ischuros* could refer to the demon.[11] If so, exorcism would involve both "binding" and "plundering." The demon must first be brought under control before his "house" (the demoniac) could be "plundered." Plundering the demons' houses, then, would mean delivering their victims, the demoniacs, from the demons that had taken up residence in them. The demoniac was thought of as the "house" (*oikos*) for his demon(s) (Matt. 12 : 44 f. = Luke 11 : 24 ff.; cf. Mark 5 : 1–16 and par.). The demons represent Satan: Satan works through the demons; the demons constitute part of Satan's "kingdom"; in effect, the demons *are* Satan. "By the prince of demons he casts out the demons," the scribes charge. Jesus responds, "How can Satan cast out *Satan*?" (v. 23). So, likewise, in v. 26: "If Satan has risen up against *himself*. . . ." The "strong man" of v. 27, then, seems to be both the demon(s) and Satan, for they are, in effect, the same. The one participates in or as the other. In either case, Jesus' activity would have been directed toward saving the lost, delivering men from Satan and his demons. Satan and his demons were now being bound.

V. 27 speaks both of plundering the strong man's *goods* and of plundering his *house*. "House" (*hē oikia*) here may refer to the demoniac, *or*, it may be parallel to Satan's *kingdom*, as in v. 25. The image of *entering* the strong man's house at the beginning of v. 27 suggests the latter—the realm of Satan. Can this, then, mean *the world*, which has been given over for a while to Satan?[12] His *house* or kingdom, then, would be plundered by carrying away his "goods" (*ta skeuē*); his *goods* would be plundered by being removed from his house. In any case, it is likely that "his goods" represent the persons who are delivered from the affliction of Satan

10. *Problem of History in Mark*, p. 35.
11. Thus H. Van der Loos, *The Miracles of Jesus* (Leiden, 1965), p. 357. It is the demon Asmodeus who is to be bound in *Tobit* 3 : 17.
12. Cf. Luke 4 : 5 f., and above, Chapter 4, note 18.

and his demons. This seems to be the understanding found in *T. Zebulon* 9 : 8 and *T. Daniel* 5 : 11 (cf. 5 : 7d). In Luke 13 : 16 Jesus speaks of loosing or unbinding (*luthēnai*) the woman whom Satan had bound (*edēsen*) for 18 years.[13] The terms "binding" (*dein*) and "loosing" or "unbinding" (*luein*) also appear in Matt. 16 : 19 and 18 : 18. Matthew evidently did not know what the saying meant, since he presented it in two separate contexts. In the first, however, it is joined to the assurance that the gates of Hades will not overpower (*katischusousin*) his followers (16 : 18b). The "gates of Hades" certainly refers to Satan and/or his demons, described in Mark 3 : 27 as the "strong" or "*power*ful man" (*ho ischuros*). Matt. 16 : 18b declares that such will not over*power* (*katischuein*) those who have received from Jesus the power of binding and loosing. Presumably it is the demons (Satan) who are to be bound, while their victims are unbound ("loosed") or "plundered." The same assurance is given in what may be a parallel recension, Luke 10 : 19, which echoes *T. Levi* 18 : 12,[14] and is implicit elsewhere, e.g., in Mark 3 : 14. Both Matt. 16 : 19 and Luke 10 : 18 f. suggest what appears elsewhere also, that history takes place on two levels. What occurs on earth has its counterpart in heaven: the defeat of Satan on earth contributes to his defeat in heaven, and vice versa.[15]

Interestingly, *T. Levi* 18 : 11b states that the "spirit of holiness" (i.e., Holy Spirit) shall be on the saints, while 12b adds explicitly that the Messiah-priest "shall give power to his children to tread upon the evil spirits." Here, as in Mark 3 : 27 ff. and Matt. 12 : 28, it is evidently by the power of the Holy Spirit that Satan and the demons are to be overcome. It is, in effect, the Holy Spirit which is at work in binding Satan and loosing his victims or plundering his spoil through the exorcisms of Jesus and his followers.

The struggle against Satan and the demons was regarded in various Jewish circles as preliminary and prerequisite to the coming of the Kingdom of God.[16] In Mark, the other synoptics, and else-

13. The same idea probably is implied in Acts 10 : 38. See Grundmann, *Markus*, p. 84: "The vessels are the possessed, who are freed by Jesus"; and *Begriff*, pp. 49 f., 69. Also Betz, "Heiliger Krieg," p. 134.

14. Also *T. Zebulon* 9 : 8; *T. Simeon* 6 : 6; and Mal. 4 : 3. Cf. Rom. 16 : 20. See below, Chapter 6.

15. Cf. Isa. 24 : 21; Eph. 6 : 12; Weiss, *Predigt*, pp. 18–22.

16. Thus Volz, *Eschatologie;* Betz, "Heiliger Krieg"; and Kee, "Terminology."

where in the NT, Satan has not yet been crushed by any means, but is still on the prowl.[17] Suffering and tribulation were still to be experienced; the Kingdom of God had not yet come (cf. *As. of Moses*, 10 : 1). But with the exorcisms effected by Jesus and his disciples through the power of the Holy Spirit, the final cosmic war had begun. The Satanic power was beginning to be bound. The culmination of this conflict would be the final defeat of Satan and the coming to earth of the Kingdom of God.[18] In the meantime, men (and women) were being freed or "loosed" from the afflictions by which Satan had sought to destroy them physically, or by undermining their faith in God. Satan's kingdom was being "plundered."

The importance of faith on the part of those healed by Jesus is a familiar though not always explicit motif, especially in Mark.[19] The faith which enables a man to be healed is the confidence that God, through Jesus, can deliver him from the evil powers. It is analogous and related to the faith of those who heed the preaching of Jesus and his disciples, trust in God's will and capacity to deliver them from the final satanic tribulation, and so are faithful and righteous to the end.[20] The mission of Jesus and his disciples was to preach and to cast out demons. Both activities have as their intent the salvation of men from Satan's destructive purposes. The "Twelve" were appointed to join with Jesus as "fishers of men" in the final effort to snatch away Satan's victims. It can be assumed that no one still possessed by a demon—thus by Satan—and/or lacking faith in God could hope to enter the Kingdom of God. Those who are healed "believe"; they trust God, and are released from their demons and thus from imprisonment in Satan's kingdom. They are no longer destined for perdition. Those who respond to the preaching by repentance, trusting God, and serving his will (Mark 3 : 35; Matt. 5 : 20; 7 : 21 ff.) are assured that they shall be received into the Kingdom of God.

Satan has been engaged in "binding" and "plundering" mankind. Now Jesus is "unbinding" them, "plundering" the plunderer,

17. E.g., John 13 : 27, 17 : 15; Acts 26 : 18; Rom. 16 : 20; II Thess. 2 : 9; I Pet. 5 : 8 f.; and Rev., *passim*.

18. So also Robinson, *Problem of History in Mark*, p. 38: "In the Markan presentation [the exorcism stories] depict a cosmic struggle in history to inaugurate the eschatological reign of God."

19. Mark 2 : 5; (4 : 40); 5 : 34; 6 : 6; (7 : 27 f.); 9 : 19, 24; Matt. 8 : 10.

20. E.g., Mark 4 : 14–20; 13 : 9 ff.; Matt. 6 : 13, 25–34; 8 : 26.

with his followers "robbing," "snatching away" the spoil, as "fishers of men" or "men of violence."[21] Through the exorcisms, Jesus is binding Satan, defeating his forces, and loosing or "plundering" his victims, liberating them for the life of fidelity to God in this age, and thus for eternal life in the age to come.

21. Luke 13 : 16; Mark 4 : 15 = Matt. 13 : 18 = Luke 8 : 12; John 10 : 12; Mark 1 : 17, cf. 3 : 14 f.; Matt. 11 : 12 (see above, Chapter 4).

6

Satan's Fall from Heaven

The seventy returned with joy, saying, "Lord, even the demons are subject to us in your name!" And he said to them, "I saw Satan fall like lightning from heaven" (Luke 10 : 17–18).

BEFORE ONE can determine the meaning of the saying, it is necessary to treat some preliminary questions. Does the vision describe something that had happened already, or was it a vision of something yet to take place? What does "fallen" (*pesonta*) mean: overcome, or come down to work evil? What is the relationship between the "fall" of Satan and Jesus' assurance to the disciples that he has given them authority or power (*exousia*) over the power of the enemy? Can the report of the vision be considered dominical, or is its authenticity—like that of the mission of "the seventy"—at best questionable?

It is usually assumed that Jesus reports a vision of an event which has already taken place: the defeat of Satan. Once this is assumed, the interpreter may speculate as to *when* Satan was defeated. Frequently interpreters of Mark 3 : 27 suppose that Jesus had earlier crushed Satan in the wilderness.[1] However, as Luke describes that scene, Satan did not "fall," but remained in command of all the Kingdoms of the earth (Luke 4 : 5–13). A few commentators have proposed that Jesus' vision was prophetic: it represented what was to take place in the future.[2] In fact, visions reported in the Biblical traditions typically are written in the past tense ("I saw"), but are prophetic of future occurrences. Thus, for example, the vision of Micaiah (I Kings 22 : 17), the various visions

1. Mark 1 : 12 f. and par.
2. E.g., Alfred Plummer, *The Gospel According to St. Luke,* ICC (New York, 1896), p. 278; Caird, *St. Luke,* p. 143.

of the prophets Amos, Jeremiah, and Ezekiel,[3] and of the seers
Daniel (Chs. 5–12) and John (Chs. 6–22).[4] Elsewhere in Luke and
the other gospels, Satan continues to be active.[5] It is, therefore,
more likely that the vision of Luke 10 : 18 referred to Satan's future
"fall" than to one posited in the past.

Such is probable, at any rate, if "fall" means defeat or ruin. There
is another possibility, however. Rev. 12 : 7–12 depicts war in
heaven, resulting in the defeat of Satan and his angels, and their
ejection thence. Satan and his angels (demons) were "thrown
down" (*eblēthēsan*) to the earth (12 : 9). They were, indeed, defeated in heaven, but those who dwell on earth must now face
Satan's final outburst of fury (12 : 12; cf. 8 : 13). Perhaps the ejection of Satan from heaven will mark the beginning of the time of
tribulation on earth.[6] Though Satan's time is short, in Rev. 12 his
arrival on earth is more like that of a cosmic paratroop division
than of a defeated general. Some interpreters have suggested that
Jesus may have meant something of this sort in Luke 10 : 18. In
that case, one would read *de* as adversative ("but") and the rest
of v. 18 as a warning against premature optimism on the part of the
disciples (v. 17); in effect, the disciples report their success against
the demons, but Jesus said to them, beware: I saw Satan come
down to reinforce his troops. Then v. 19 would represent Jesus' assurance that *despite* Satan's arrival (whether past or prospective),
his followers will nevertheless prevail against "all power of the
enemy."[7] It is likely that Luke and the other synoptic evangelists
continued to expect the time of tribulation in the near future.
Clearly they reported sayings of Jesus which indicate that he expected it (together with the appearance of the Messiah, the arrival
of the Kingdom of God, and the time of Judgment) during the
lifetime of his own contemporaries. But this does not tell us

3. E.g., Amos 7 : 1 ff., 8 : 1; cf. 5 : 2; Jer. 1 : 13 ff., 24 : 1 ff.; Ezek.
12 : 21–28, 37 : 1 ff.
4. Note esp. Rev. 20 : 10.
5. E.g., Luke 22 : 3, 31. Though Luke's version of the "Lord's Prayer"
does not mention the "Evil One," it does refer to the threat of "temptation"
(*peirasmos*) and the activity of "the devil" continues to be expected according to Luke 8 : 12 which Luke preserves from Mark.
6. Cf. Mark 13 = Matt. 24 = Luke 21. Or, it may mark the *end* of the
time of tribulation: Mark 13 : 25b and par.
7. Cf. Luke 12 : 32, 21 : 18 f.; also Matt. 16 : 18. Schlätter finds a close
parallel between Luke 10 : 18 f. and 22 : 31 f., but sees both in terms of the
courtroom rather than cosmic dualism: Adolf Schlätter, *Das Evangelium des
Lukas*, 2d ed. (Stuttgart, 1960), pp. 279 f.

whether in Luke 10 : 18 Jesus visualized Satan's arrival in power, or his defeat.

It would help if we knew whether Satan's fall landed him on earth or in Hades. In Rev. 12, Satan is expelled *to the earth* (12 : 9, 12) where he will work his wrath in the time that remains. In Luke 10 : 15, however, Jesus declares that Capernaum will be brought down *to Hades*. Luke's account in 10 : 13–24 seems to be following the tradition Matthew reports in 11 : 20–26. Luke, who is not above linking his material together on the basis of word association (cf. "rejoice" and "spirit" in 10 : 20, 21), may have chosen to insert the return of the seventy and the report of Jesus' vision here because bringing Capernaum to Hades—instead of to heaven (v. 15)— brought to mind the prospective fate of Satan. In this case, we might understand Luke to have meant that Jesus visualized Satan's ultimate defeat and condemnation. Such, of course, is expected also in the Apocalypse: note especially Rev. 14 : 8 and 18 : 2 where the same verb (*piptein*) is used to describe the (prospective) fall of "Babylon" as that which appears in speaking of Satan's "fall" in Luke 10 : 18! See also Isa. 14 : 12–15 which refers in the "prophetic perfect" to the prospective fall of the king of Babylon from heaven to Sheol. The same verb is used in the LXX at Isa. 21 : 9, and would have been known to Luke. Whether Luke also knew its use in the Apocalypse of John is not certain. John the seer looked forward to the time when Satan would finally be thrown down (*eblēthē*) into the lake of fire (Rev. 20 : 7–10). Jesus himself may have been capable of visualizing the torment of the damned in the fire of hell (Gehenna), as in Mark 9 : 43–48, even if Luke preferred to de-emphasize such features. How much more might Jesus have visualized the fate of "the Evil One" himself, Satan! The balance of probability seems to weigh slightly in favor of the assumption that 10 : 18 describes Satan's ultimate defeat, rather than his inauguration of the period of final "woes" on earth.

In that case, what is the relation between vv. 18 and 19? Those who assume that Satan has already been defeated see a causal relationship: because Satan has been defeated, Jesus' followers can now deal with the evil spirits or satanic powers.[8] But if so, why should Jesus need to assure them that he was *now* conferring special authority or power upon them? It seems that Jesus was arming

---

8. Cf. the assumption that Mark 3 : 27 means that because Jesus had earlier "bound" Satan, he can now "plunder" his household through exorcisms.

his band of followers in preparation for future dealings with demonic or satanic forces. Something of the sort may be the meaning
also of Matt. 16 : 18b–19; the "gates of Hades" obviously means
demonic forces, and "binding" and "loosing" certainly are suggestive
of exorcism.[9] As has been noted earlier, Satan reappears later on in
Luke: he had not yet been bound or "fallen" in such a way as to
cease being a menace to Jesus and his followers. Another possibility is to view vv. 18 and 19 as parallel statements, the one equivalent to the other: the exercise of power against the demons means
that Satan is being defeated. Such, perhaps, is the understanding
of the author of the *Testament of Levi* 18 : 12, from which v. 19
may be derived.[10] In this poem the writer makes a series of evidently parallel statements (see esp. vv. 3–4, 7–14), including v. 12:

> And Beliar shall be bound by him,
> And he shall give power to His children to tread upon the
> evil spirits.[11]

Again, the meaning may be causal, but in a converse sense: because Jesus' followers have power "over all the power of the
enemy," Jesus' confidence in Satan's prospective defeat is confirmed. Professor Creed favors the first explanation: "The defeat
of Satan explains the success of the disciples. Jesus has given them
authority over all the powers of evil."[12] But Creed's second statement, which accurately represents the meaning of v. 19, could
equally describe the second or third possibility: the authority
granted by Jesus to the disciples (here, to the "seventy") explains
the fact that Satan is being defeated, or, justifies the expectation of
his final overthrow. Before trying to resolve this basic question,
some attention should be given to the verse's authenticity and to
that of its context.

The mission of the "seventy" probably should be regarded as a

---

9. Matthew construed the saying to sanction the prerogatives of Peter in
the early Church. The saying does not appear in Mark, but may have been in
"Q" in a form more like that found in Luke 10 : 19.

10. Unless the passage in *T. Levi* represents a Christian revision based
upon Jesus' saying.

11. The quotation in 10 : 19, however, may follow Psalm 91 : 13, which
speaks of "serpents" rather than "evil spirits."

12. John M. Creed, *The Gospel According to St. Luke* (London, 1957),
p. 147.

Lukan invention.[13] Several features of it correspond a bit too nicely with Luke's theory that from the first Christianity was meant for the gentiles. The number seventy (or seventy-two) probably was meant to represent the total number of nations in the world, and thus symbolize (and authenticate) the later gentile mission which Luke elsewhere was obviously desirous of justifying.[14] Browning sees a parallel between the twelve and seventy in Luke 9, 10 on the one hand, and the twelve and seven in Acts. The seven leaders of the gentile Christians in Acts 6[15] replace the "seventy" of Luke 10.[16] Luke omits the limitation of the mission to the "house" or "towns" of Israel (cf. Matt. 10 : 5 f., 23);[17] but he adds that the missionaries are to eat and drink what is offered them, a seemingly insignificant detail, but one which means that they may properly ignore Jewish dietary restrictions, thus implying a mission upon gentile soil (cf. Acts 10–11). Luke states that the missionaries were sent out two-by-two, thereby further anticipating the pattern of the later mission to the gentiles.[18] Possibly it is significant that *T. Levi* 18 from which Luke 10 : 19 may be derived also contemplates the enlightenment of the gentiles (18 : 9).

The purpose of their mission, as Luke presents it, is not so much to extend Jesus' own ministry of healing and proclaiming the imminence of the Kingdom, as to prepare the way for Jesus' own appearance in the towns and places along his route. Luke retains the eschatological message and urgency which he derives from "Q,"[19] but since the missionaries are to return from this mission prior to the parousia of the Son of man (cf. Matt. 10 : 23), and

13. Its authenticity has been defended recently: Tinsley, *Luke*, p. 113.

14. Thus Caird, *St. Luke*, p. 144; cf. Plummer, *St. Luke*, pp. 269 f., who notes other types of significance associated with the number seventy.

15. See Walther Schmithals, *Paul and James*, SBT no. 46 (Naperville, Ill., 1965), pp. 16–37.

16. W. R. F. Browning, *The Gospel According to Saint Luke* (London, 1960), pp. 109 f.

17. It is also possible that Matthew added it from a source unknown to Luke.

18. See Tinsley, *Luke*, p. 113. Or, Luke may have simply taken this feature from Mark 6 : 7. Jeremias suggests that Jesus in fact did send out his followers two-by-two: Joachim Jeremias, *Abba* (Göttingen, 1966), pp. 132–39.

19. Cf. Matt. 10 : 7–15. To this Luke adds that they are to lose no time along the road with pleasantries (10 : 4b). Thus Burton Easton, *The Gospel According to St. Luke* (New York, 1926), p. 157. Perhaps this detail was in "Q." There seems no reason for Luke to have invented it, and it accords with the urgency of the disciples' mission and message.

merely anticipate Jesus' presumed later journey through the countryside (of Galilee and Samaria?), the significance of their message and urgency becomes obscure.[20] The mission becomes (for Luke) symbolic of the later gentile mission, rather than the final call to repentance which it was in the "Q" tradition; for Luke, of course, was quite aware that the Kingdom of God had not come during Jesus' lifetime.

The saying reported in Luke 10 : 18 is not dependent upon the mission of the seventy. It does, however, presuppose some such setting as that given in v. 17b: some (if not all "seventy") of his disciples report success in exorcising demons. The use of the imperfect (*etheōroun* ["I saw"]) in v. 18 does not tell us when Jesus had the vision—it may have been as the disciples were speaking of their success, or earlier. It is not possible to tell whether the report inspired the vision, or whether the report confirmed what an earlier vision had intimated, the eventual downfall of Satan. But, in any case, the success against the demons implies the substance of the vision. Such also was the case in Matt. 12 : 28 = Luke 11 : 20: if it is by God's spirit that Jesus casts out the demons, *then* (*ara*) the Pharisees should recognize that the Kingdom of God is near. Possibly the healings wrought by Jesus, reported in Luke 17 : 11–19, did prompt them to inquire when the Kingdom was coming (17 : 20a). To some, Jesus' healings and/or exorcisms suggested that he was Elijah, the forerunner of the Messianic Age (Mark 6 : 13–15; Matt. 11 : 2 f. = Luke 7 : 18 f.). The work of exorcism seems to have been recognized as preliminary and preparatory to the coming of the Kingdom of God.

Certainly the Kingdom of God would not be established on earth until Satan has finally been overthrown or bound. Thus those who pray for the coming of the Kingdom also pray that in the meantime God will deliver them from the power of the Evil One (Matt. 6 : 10, 13). Similarly, in Mark 3 : 22–30, Jesus explains to the Pharisees that Satan's Kingdom is coming to an end, not because of civil war in Satan's household, but because the Holy Spirit is operative in his exorcisms. By defeating the demons, Jesus is

20. Proponents of "realized eschatology," of course, try to account for this urgency on some basis other than belief that the Kingdom of God was near: e.g., Caird, *St. Luke*, p. 143: "The time is short because the opposition is gathering its forces."

binding the strong man, Satan, and thus preparing for the coming of the Kingdom of God.[21] Perhaps, as has been suggested, such a meaning is also implied in Jesus' statement about the Kingdom's "coming violently": the healing wrought by Jesus and his followers (Matt. 11 : 4 f., but not here designated as exorcism) causes the Kingdom to come (Matt. 11 : 12)[22] or, at all events, prepares the earth for its coming by defeating the forces of evil which have hitherto reigned here. This seems to be the understanding implicit in the instructions recorded in 10 : 9–12. The task of healing the sick is combined with that of proclaiming the message that the Kingdom has come near. Those who respond to the mission of the disciples will be ready for the Kingdom when it comes. But woe to those who do not. "On that day"—the day when the Kingdom and Judgment (v. 14) are actualized—the unrepentant towns will suffer a fate more severe than that in store for the resurrected dead of wicked old Sodom (v. 12).

It is possible, as has often been proposed, that the meaning of Luke 10 : 18 (and, in effect, of Mark 3 : 27 and Matt. 12 : 28 = Luke 11 : 20) is that exorcisms can be performed because Satan has been defeated and the Kingdom is present.[23] But since elsewhere in the synoptic tradition Satan continues to be active and the coming of the Kingdom is regularly regarded as a future event, it seems more plausible to conclude that the meaning is as the other evidence noted also suggests: Jesus understood that through his own success and that of his disciples against the demons, Satan's power is being overcome. Satan's Kingdom will at last come to an end; his hold upon the earth is being broken and soon the Kingdom of God will be established over the earth.

21. J. M. Robinson opposes the theory, earlier advocated by Klostermann and Wendland (that "binding" corresponds to "exorcism," and "plundering" to the "parousia"), because, in Robinson's judgment, "the exorcisms are not causal presuppositions of the parousia" (*Problem of History in Mark,* p. 31n1). But would the Kingdom of God be established on earth while Satan still rules here? See Kee, "Terminology," 232–46, and above, Chs. 3–5.

22. See above, Ch. 4.

23. It is not correct to speak, as many do, of the presence of the "powers of the Kingdom of God" in connection with Jesus' exorcisms. That expression does not appear in the synoptic tradition. It is the power of the Holy Spirit or of God that was thought operative: Matt. 12 : 28, 31 f.; Mark 3 : 28 f.; Luke 11 : 20; cf. 10 : 21.

7

The Greatest of Those Born of Women

Truly, I say to you, among those born of women there has risen no one greater than John the Baptist; yet he who is least in the kingdom of heaven is greater than he (Matt. 11 : 11 = Luke 7 : 28).

THE VERSE in question has been understood by many critics to mean that Jesus believed that some in his time had already entered the Kingdom of God. If so, the Kingdom of God would have been, in some way, present.[1] But this meaning is not so obvious as these writers suppose. It contains some riddles. Why is not the greatest of all men (John the Baptist) in the Kingdom? Who, if anyone, is not born of women but is in the Kingdom? What does Jesus' identification of John as *Elijah* have to do with the meaning of the verse? What should those with ears to hear, hear (11 : 14)?

Also, the authenticity of at least half of the verse is in question. Many interpreters read the second half of the verse as a reflection of later rivalry or animosity between John's disciples and Jesus', and thus as originating among the latter in order to put the former in their place.[2] Those who are in the Kingdom of God are, on this theory, members of the Christian Church. The least of them is greater than John the Baptist: how much more so, then, than John's latter-day disciples! If this explanation is correct, the second part of the verse would tell us nothing about whether Jesus thought the Kingdom present or future. The first half of the verse would remain, however, meaning simply that Jesus thought of John as the greatest man who had ever lived.[3] Exegesis of the verse would be obliged to end at this point.

1. E.g., de Dietrich, *Matthew*, p. 70; Tinsley, *Luke*, p. 79; Ladd, *Jesus and the Kingdom*, pp. 119, 193 ff.
2. Kümmel, *Promise and Fulfilment*, p. 125n75. So also Easton, *St. Luke*, p. 102; Oscar Cullmann, *The Early Church* (Philadelphia, 1956), p. 127, who traces this theory ultimately to W. Baldensperger.
3. Cf. Walter E. Bundy, *The Religion of Jesus* (Indianapolis, 1928), p. 48.

It is not necessary, however, to suppose a hypothetical rivalry between early Baptists and Christians in order to account for the second half of the verse.[4] If the half verse is secondary, it is just as plausible to regard it as one of those adjustments in the tradition which was felt necessary in order to avoid what otherwise would be a theological embarrassment: the Baptist is hailed by Jesus (who was born of woman) as the greatest of those born of women. The Christian tradition wishes to make it clear that Jesus, whom it now acknowledges as the Christ and Lord, if not son of God, is (or was) really the greatest.[5] But if the whole verse should be attributed to Jesus, what then would have been his meaning?

It has been proposed that Jesus spoke these words in order to rebuke the Baptist for his (nowhere evident) political messianism,[6] or for preaching the demand for repentance instead of proclaiming the good news of salvation, or for some other conjectured fault.[7] But did Jesus intend here to rebuke the Baptist? He had sought baptism at John's hands; preached the same message as John;[8] had just acknowledged John to be both "prophet" and "more than a prophet," God's "messenger" (11 : 9 f.); was about to identify John explicitly as Elijah (11 : 14); associated John's rejection at the hands of "this generation" with his own (11 : 15–19; cf. Mark 9 : 12 f.); and again, near the end of his ministry, linked the question of his own authority with that of John's (21 : 24–27, 32). In none of these places is there any hint that Jesus wished to reprove or dissociate himself from John. Why should Jesus rebuke God's messenger, "the coming one" (*ho erchomenos*), Elijah—even if John did not know that he himself was the fulfiller of that role— who, so far as we can tell, had performed his mission faultlessly? Jesus does not at any point rebuke (*epitiman*) John, though he re-

4. That this hypothesis is no longer tenable has been shown by J. A. T. Robinson, "Elijah, John and Jesus" in his *Twelve New Testament Studies*, SBT no. 34 (London, 1962), pp. 49 ff. So also Schniewind, *Matthäus*, p. 143.

5. Cf. Matthew's reworking of Mark 10 : 17 f., or the treatment of Jesus' baptism in the later gospels, e.g., Matt. 3 : 13–15. Thus also William C. Robinson, Jr., *Der Weg des Herrn* (Hamburg-Bergstedt, 1964), p. 19.

6. Thus, e.g., Johannes Weiss.

7. E.g., F. C. Grant in *Nelson's Bible Commentary*, vi (New York, 1962), p. 64: "John never recognized Jesus as Messiah, and therefore he was still outside the kingdom."

8. Namely, "Repent, the Kingdom of God has come near (*ēngiken*)." Cf. Mark 1 : 15 = Matt. 4 : 17; Matt. 10 : 7; Luke 10 : 9, 11; 21 : 31; and Matt. 3 : 2.

bukes several others, including Peter. Why, then, should John be differentiated from those in the Kingdom of God?

The answer seems simple, but because it is obvious, it is not necessarily incorrect: John is not in the Kingdom of God because, as (*ho erchomenos*), "the coming one" who would appear *before* the great and terrible day of the Lord comes (Mal. 4 : 5), he necessarily *precedes* the arrival of the Kingdom of God. The Kingdom of God is not present because Elijah, who was to come first, is. John (Elijah) is not in the Kingdom of God because the Kingdom of God has not yet come!

Far from rebuking John, Jesus pays him the highest of compliments: he is the greatest of those born of women (11 : 11a). Luke reports that "all of the people and the tax collectors" understood Jesus' words as an endorsement of John and his baptizing (Luke 7 : 29). And yet, such is the difference between the Kingdom of Heaven and the present age, that even the least of those in the Kingdom is greater than even the greatest man of the present age.

A point generally overlooked by those who hold that here Jesus implies that some are already in the Kingdom is that in every other place where those in the Kingdom of God are ranked as greatest and least, first and last, those so ranked are not yet in the Kingdom of God. How they *will be* ranked there depends upon their present response to God and men.[9] Why is the least in the Kingdom greater than John? Because anyone *then* and *there* is greater than anyone *here* and *now*. The fundamental comparison is not between John and his contemporaries, or between the greatest and least of those who are or will be in the Kingdom of Heaven, but between *those born of women* (*en gennētois gunaikōn*), i.e., those living in the present age,[10] and *those in the Kingdom of Heaven* (*en tē basileia tōn ouranōn*). No tense is indicated in the first part of the clause: the words *ho de mikroteros en tē basileia tōn ouranōn* can equally mean "he who is in the Kingdom of Heaven" and "he who will be" there. In Hebrew and Aramaic, the present and future tenses are indistinguishable, and the verb "to be" frequently omitted. The Greek verb *estin* can represent the Aramaic "will be" *and* "is."[11]

9. Matt. 5 : 19, 18 : 1–4; Mark 10 : 31 = Matt. 19 : 30; Matt. 20 : 16.

10. That Jesus thought his disciples and other contemporaries were still living in the old world, the present age, is apparent elsewhere, e.g.: Mark 10 : 30; Matt. 12 : 32, 19 : 28; Luke 18 : 30, 20 : 34 f. Such is Matthew's viewpoint also: e.g., Matt. 28 : 20.

11. Thus M'Neile, *St. Matthew*, p. 154. Cf. Luke 17 : 21.

It is not unlikely that the meaning of the half verse, if authentic, is this: ". . . but the least in the Kingdom of Heaven will be greater (then) than John is (now)." What would have been the existential relevance of such an observation? It would be the same point as in much of the rest of Jesus' "teaching": the Kingdom of God is the most important matter; for it, his hearers must give up all other security and treasures, and make themselves ready for this decisive imminent event. The crowds have gone out from curiosity to see John, and now they flock after Jesus (11 : 7–9). But more than curiosity is needed if they are to survive the day of judgment, namely, repentance—faith in God, seeking the Kingdom, and a life of moral seriousness.[12]

It is possible, of course, that Jesus really did mean that some already were in the Kingdom of Heaven. If so, who was not born of women, who therefore might be in the Kingdom of Heaven? Two answers seem possible.

The first possibility is that no one born *only* of woman could enter the Kingdom of Heaven. Being born of woman is not enough: one must be born *again* in some way, and this second birth or re-birth would distinguish a person from those born *only* of women. Such seems to be the meaning of John 3 : 3–5: "Truly, I say to you, unless one is born anew, he cannot see the Kingdom of God." This Johannine saying bears a striking resemblance to Matt. 18 : 3. In both the expression *eiselthein eis* ("enter into") occurs, and in the Sinaiticus reading of John 3 : 5, the Mattheanesque *tōn ouranōn* ("of heaven") is found. Both passages begin with the emphatic *amēn legō* ("truly I say") (cf. Matt. 11 : 11), and both declare that in order to enter (see) the Kingdom of God (Heaven), one must be born anew or again (John) or become again like little children (Matthew). Even the basic verbs are similar in sound and appearance: *genēsthe* ("become"), *gennēthē* ("is born").[13] The verb *strephein* ("to turn") in Matt. 18 : 3 and the Johannine setting (3 : 3–21) both suggest that the essential meaning in each case is the necessity of conversion. In that case, the meaning here would

---

12. Matt. 11 : 16–24; see also 6 : 19–33, 7 : 21 (cf. 25 : 44!); Mark 3 : 31–35; Luke 11 : 27 f.

13. The Fourth Evangelist may have adapted the Matthean saying with slight, if hyperbolic, modification. Mark 10 : 15 = Luke 18 : 17 should also be considered as possible recensions of such a saying.

be the same, in effect, as in Mark 1 : 15 = Matt. 4 : 17 and in nearly
every other synoptic passage where the verb *metanoein* ("to repent") occurs: those who would enter the Kingdom of God must
"turn," or "repent."[14]

It may be, however, that Matt. 18 : 3 and John 3 : 3, 5 indicate
not only a spiritual rebirth or conversion, but also a quasi-physical
new birth or re-creation as prerequisite to entering or seeing the
Kingdom of God, as in I Cor. 15 : 50 ff. In Matt. 19 : 28 and I Cor.
15, such a new birth or re-creation was thought of as part of the
miraculous transformation of the cosmos that would take place as
the present world (both heaven and earth) passes away, and is
succeeded by the "new world" or the Coming Age.[15] This expectation or hope appears in the OT as early as Isa. 65 : 17 ff.: "For behold, I create new heavens and a new earth . . ." (also 66 : 22).

The universal rebirth (*palingenesia*) mentioned in Matt. 19 : 28,
of course, will take place in the future: it will be the time "when
the Son of man shall sit on his glorious throne" in Judgment. Reference to the expected "birth pangs" (*ōdin*) in Mark 13 : 8 = Matt.
24 : 8 is also suggestive of the "birth" of the Messianic Age.[16] Paul
uses the future tense in speaking both of the resurrection and of
the "change" which he and those others who, he thought, would
still be alive were to experience at the sound of the last trumpet,[17]
even though he speaks of those "in Christ" as being already a "new
creature" or "creation" (II Cor. 5 : 17; cf. Gal. 6 : 15).

It may be that the meaning of Matt. 11 : 11 is that John the Baptist, and all others still living during the days of the present age
who are, necessarily, born *only* of women, must be born again,
either in the sense of repentance or conversion, or by participating
physically in the general *palingenesia* ("second birth") in which
all things and all persons will be made new, or in both senses. If
so, there would, as yet, be no one in the Kingdom of Heaven;[18]
those who were to experience "rebirth" at the beginning of the New

14. See Bauer, *Lexicon*, pp. 513 f. on *metanoeō* and *metanoia*.
15. So also Schniewind, *Matthäus*, cf. Rom. 8 : 22; I Cor. 7 : 31.
16. See Joseph Klausner, *The Messianic Idea in Israel* (New York, 1955),
pp. 440 ff. On *palingenesia* see Bauer, *Lexicon*, p. 611.
17. I Cor. 15 : 51–53; also I Thess. 4 : 15–17; cf. Matt. 24 : 31; Isa. 27 : 13.
18. Even if only a spiritual rebirth was in view, there is no suggestion in
synoptic tradition that anyone had already been "born again" in that sense.
Some may have repented, but this would not mean that they were already in
the Kingdom of God.

Age would *afterwards* be greater than John is now, even though he is the greatest man of the present age. There is, so to speak, an infinite qualitative distinction between life in the present age and that in the Kingdom of God such that the least in the Age to Come will be greater in blessings or purity of heart than even the greatest or most righteous man of the present era.

However plausible the foregoing interpretation of 11 : 11 may be, it should be noted that the verse does not read "among those born *only* of women" but, simply, "among those born of women." As the text stands, the contrast is between those born of women and those in the Kingdom of Heaven. It is implied that these two categories are mutually exclusive, at least in the present time. Are there any who have *not* been born of women, who might, consequently, already be in the Kingdom of Heaven?[19] Angels are not mentioned here explicitly, nor are they in Matt. 6 : 10. But who else does the will of the Father already *in heaven,* while the disciples, on earth, still pray for the coming of the Kingdom, the time when the Father's will also will be done (by men) on earth? The idea of the heavenly "Council" (*sōd*) of angelic beings goes back into OT times (e.g., Isa. 6 : 1–8; Job. 1 : 6 ff.; Tobit 3 : 16 f.).

There are more references to angels than to demons in the synoptic gospels. The angels (like the demons) seem to have had a real place in the cosmology of Jesus and his contemporaries. The angels are now in heaven, neither marrying nor being given in marriage.[20] How, under these circumstances, the species is generated is not

---

19. It may have been thought that some of the great men of the past were now alive in heaven: notably, Enoch (cf. Gen. 5 : 24), Moses (the title *The Assumption of Moses,* if not the story), Elijah (II Kings 2 : 11), and the patriarchs. The "transfiguration" (Mark 9 : 4 ff.) implies belief at least in the early Church that Moses and Elijah were alive in heaven. In Luke 16 : 19–31 father Abraham is pictured, presumably in heaven, among the living. Perhaps it was supposed that the patriarchs had entered heaven without needing first to pass through Judgment, since their exceptional favor with God could be assumed. In Mark 12 : 18–27 = Matt. 22 : 23–33 it seems that Abraham, Isaac, and Jacob are among the dead who will be raised at the time of the Resurrection; but the Lukan parallel hints that they may be among those who already "live to" God (Luke 20 : 38). Jewish tradition pictures several figures of antiquity living in Paradise: e.g., Elijah, Enoch, and even Jonah. Thus Billerbeck, IV, pt. 2, 784 f.; Louis Ginzberg, *The Legends of the Jews* (Philadelphia, 1913), IV, 253; and Klausner, *Messianic Idea,* p. 466. All of these, however, presumably had been "born of women."

20. Mark 12 : 25 = Matt. 22 : 30. Cf. Gen. 6 : 1–4.

stated, but presumably they were not understood to have been born of women! When men participate in the resurrection and enter the Kingdom of Heaven, they will then become like the angels, neither marrying nor giving in marriage—though, Paul suggests, love need not then cease (I Cor. 13 : 8–13!)—and doing the will of the heavenly Father.

It would appear to be a truism to say that John the Baptist, though the greatest among those born of women, is not so great as the least of the angels in heaven. Yet this may have been exactly what Jesus meant. If so, the basic contrast in the verse would be not only temporal—between the present period of "the forerunner" (*ho erchomenos*) of the Messianic Age in which even the greatest of men still awaits rebirth at the *palingenesia* ("second genesis") on the one hand, and the future state of those in the Kingdom of Heaven on the other—but also spatial: between those now living on earth, and the life of the angels now in heaven. It is quite likely that the Kingdom of God was thought of as being present, spatially, overhead. When the Kingdom of God comes on earth in the future, it will come down.[21] Then, following the resurrection (Mark 12 : 25 = Matt. 22 : 30), men also will become like the angels. Not only the resurrected dead, but all others as well who are to enter the Kingdom will experience a new birth.

It is probably only coincidental that one tradition reports Jesus' having identified the Baptist as the "angel" (*angelos*) of God in the preceding verse (11 : 10 = Luke 7 : 27), quoting from Mal. 3 : 1. There the term *mal'ach* is used, which in that context probably should be translated as "messenger," "herald," or "prophet" rather than as "angel." Evidently, John is not one of the *angeloi* who are in heaven—although Elijah had been carried to heaven according to II Kings 2 : 11—and he was, reportedly, born of woman (Luke 1). If, however, John is the messenger or prophet who was to come to prepare the way for the Lord, to cause the people to repent before the great and terrible day of the Lord comes,[22] neither he nor any of his contemporaries could have entered the Kingdom of Heaven, for it had not yet come. It was not yet time for "those born of women" to enter, but it was time for them to prepare for the coming of the Kingdom of God and the Son of man by re-

21. Mark 13 : 26, 14 : 62, and par.; Matt. 6 : 10; cf. Rev. 21 : 2.
22. Mal. 4 : 6 (= 3 : 34, Heb.); Ecclus. 48 : 10; Matt. 17 : 10–12. Cf. the message of John in Mark 1 : 4 = Matt. 3 : 1.

pentance. Otherwise they would have no share in the blessed life which the angels already enjoy. Jesus may have intended a comparison between the situation of the angel-messenger John (Elijah) on earth where the Kingdom had not yet come, and that of the angels in heaven where the Kingdom was already established.

Strangely, interpreters who cite 11 : 11 as evidence that the Kingdom of God was thought to be present generally pass over the first half of the verse in silence. The fact that Jesus praises the Baptist over all those others born of women—a fairly inclusive category—usually is unnoticed or unexplained. Scant if any attention is paid to the decisive phrase *en gennētois gunaikōn* ("among those born of women"). And yet, if part of the verse is secondary, it is the *second* half verse, the so-called rebuke. If the verse as a whole is authentic, and the first half is taken into account rather than simply ignored, it is difficult to see how the verse can be construed to mean that Jesus thought that some men had already entered the Kingdom of God.

Many interpreters go to great pains to urge that Jesus could not really have meant that the Baptist was to be excluded from the Kingdom, after all. T. W. Manson, for instance, resorts to the improbable speculation that Jesus thought the Kingdom would come twice or in two stages. John was excluded from "its present manifestation," but would be included when it was "fully realized in the future."[23] However commendable this concern for the Baptist's ultimate fate may be, it rests upon the questionable assumption that Jesus declared John excluded from the Kingdom of God while other mortals (offspring of women) had already been admitted to it.

The more likely meaning, given the fact that Jesus identified the Baptist as the prophet and more-than-prophet Elijah who must come first (Matt. 11 : 13 f., 17 : 10 ff.), is that the final time *before* the coming of the Kingdom of God has come. When the Kingdom of God comes, even the least of those who then share its blessings will surpass the greatest of the men of the former age, even the final messenger of God to the old world, Elijah, John the Baptist. For then, all who are to enter the Kingdom—including,

23. *The Sayings of Jesus* (London, 1949), p. 70; also Caird, *St. Luke,* p. 112.

we may assume, the Baptist—will have been transformed, and all will enjoy the infinitely greater blessings of life in the Messianic Age (cf. Matt. 5 : 3–12). But *only* those who recognize the times, who perceive that God has sent Elijah, and respond with repentance to the deeds and message which Jesus and his disciples also perform and proclaim, will have a share in those blessings.[24] It was not a time for curiosity, but for conversion (cf. Luke 13 : 1–5).

24. Matt. 10 : 5–15, 11 : 12–24.

8

The Urgent Mission of the Twelve

When they persecute you in one town, flee to the next; for truly, I say to you, you will not have gone through all the towns of Israel, before the Son of man comes (Matt. 10 : 23).

THE FACT that this saying was not fulfilled has troubled interpreters who find it uncomfortable to suppose that the NT tradition could have been capable of error. Oscar Cullmann, for instance, who fears that the primitive Christian hope "falls" if that hope referred to an early date, declares that the meaning of 10 : 23 (and also of Mark 9 : 1 and 13 : 30) "is not clear" and that, besides, their importance has been exaggerated.[1] The meaning of the verse, however, could not be clearer: Jesus tells the twelve that the Son of man will have come before they complete their mission through the towns of Israel. Floyd Filson asserts that Matthew and the early Church "certainly" could not have thought that Jesus was mistaken; consequently, he attributes to Matthew a distinction between the preliminary but "real coming" of the Son of man and his subsequent "full and final manifestation," so that Matthew's Jesus was not mistaken after all: "As the Apostles do the works of Christ and win men to accept his Kingdom message, the Kingdom comes and the Son of man is manifested."[2] Several other writers evidently prefer the belief that the Church should have been mistaken rather than the view that Jesus himself had been in error about this. At any rate, many commentators treat the saying as secondary, i.e., attribute it to the early Church rather than to Jesus—e.g., Norman Perrin and R. H. Fuller.[3] It is proposed that the saying was created by the post-Easter community to reassure itself that salvation was

1. *Christ and Time*, rev. ed. (Philadelphia, 1964), pp. 87 f.
2. *The Gospel According to St. Matthew* (New York, 1960), pp. 131 f.
3. Perrin, *Rediscovering the Teaching of Jesus* (New York, 1967), pp. 201 f.; Fuller, *Foundations*, p. 147.

66

near. But why then is it placed in the context of Jesus' instructions to the twelve, in connection with their mission undertaken *during* his lifetime? Why was it not included in the instructions of the risen Lord for the post-Easter mission (28 : 16 ff.)?

Suspicion that the verse may be secondary is not completely unfounded. Matt. 10 : 17–22, which comes with only slight alteration from Mark 13 : 9–13, probably reflects the experience of the early Christian community. Reference to bearing testimony before the gentiles is more reminiscent of situations depicted in Acts and the letters of Paul than any we know of during Jesus' lifetime; furthermore, it is out of place beside Jesus' (Matthew's?) restriction of the mission to the "house of Israel" (10 : 5 f.). It may be that 10 : 23a also reflects subsequent Christian experience of persecution at the hands of Jews and/or gentiles. This is not so certain, however, for persecution is not an unusual experience for those who call upon people to repent.[4] Elsewhere Jesus reportedly promised his companions that they could expect to be persecuted (e.g., Mark 10 : 30; Matt. 5 : 10 f.). Possibly such anticipated persecution was associated with the final effort of Satan to hold the world in subjection to his dominion.[5] The persecution referred to in 10 : 23a may be related to the "unworthy" reception that Jesus warned the twelve they would encounter (10 : 12–15).

Reference to persecution in v. 23 could well be secondary. It would not follow, however, that the verse as a whole is secondary. Its substance corresponds closely with the tradition in 10 : 5–15(16), the authenticity of which is not in serious doubt. In vv. 5–15, the twelve are to move from town to town performing exorcisms and proclaiming that the Kingdom of God has come near (*ēngiken*). In v. 23 they are told that when they meet with hostile response in one town, they should "flee to the next," for the Son of man will come before they have completed their mission through all the towns of Israel. In fact, v. 23 closely parallels, if not follows directly (in thought), vv. 14 f. The day of judgment is coming

4. Cf. de Dietrich, *Matthew*, p. 68, and the fate of numerous civil rights leaders in the United States.
5. Matt. 6 : 13, 11 : 12, 13 : 38; see above, Chs. 3–6. Note Matt. 10 : 8 where the disciples are charged to continue the campaign against Satan's house, the demons; and the reference to "wolves" in 10 : 16. Cf. Matt. 7 : 15, 13 : 19; and John 10 : 12, 28.

(10 : 15); the coming of the Son of man is near (10 : 23). The "instructions" in 10 : 5–14, and also the verses that introduce the section (9 : 37 f. = Luke 10 : 2), suggest that haste is necessary because time is short.[6] Reference to the harvest (a traditional image for the messianic age) in 9 : 37 f. corresponds not only to the message of the twelve that the Kingdom of God is near (ēngiken) (10 : 7), but also to the expected "day of judgment" (10 : 15), and the coming of the Son of man (10 : 23). Jesus, himself, teaches and heals in the cities and villages, has compassion on the leaderless masses (9 : 35 f.), and is concerned that many of them may fail to be included in the coming "harvest" because they are unaware of the decisive times and are still bound by Satan (10 : 7–8a). Therefore Jesus sends out the twelve to extend his own work of preaching and exorcism, hastening through as many of the towns of Israel as they can before the coming of the Son of man, time of judgment, and Kingdom of God. The limitation of the mission of the twelve to the towns of Israel in 10 : 23 corresponds to the instructions given in 10 : 5 f. It seems likely, therefore, that 10 : 23, with the possible exception of its reference to persecution, belongs in the context of 9:35–10:16, namely, with Jesus' other instructions to his disciples with regard to their urgent mission to Israel during his lifetime.[7]

The mission of the twelve corresponds to the program of Jesus' ministry and the work of his followers as we have seen it elsewhere in the synoptic tradition. By preaching that the Kingdom of God is at hand they warn men that they now have their last opportunity to choose between God and other masters, for only those found faithful to God (and his righteousness) can hope to enter his Kingdom. By healing or exorcism, they loose men from the bondage of Satan or the demons, a bondage that afflicts them not only in the present age, but is intended for their ultimate destruction. In both preaching and exorcism, Jesus and his followers are "fishers of men," seeking to rescue them from Satan's clutches and free them for the Kingdom of God. They are binding the demons (or Satan) and

6. So also Dom Jacques Dupont, " 'Vous n'aurez pas achevé les villes d'Israel avant que le fils de l'homme ne vienne' (Matt. 10 : 23)," *NT* 2 (1958), 231, 236; also Filson, *St. Matthew*, p. 130.

7. Contrary to Kümmel's view that it is a detached logion. But Kümmel does regard the verse, like Mark 9 : 1 and 13 : 30, as authentic (*Promise and Fulfilment*, pp. 61–67).

loosing their victims, plundering Satan's Kingdom, gathering for the harvest.[8]

The limitation of the mission to the towns of Israel (10 : 23) has been regarded by some interpreters as a secondary feature. It is generally recognized that Matthew presents a picture in which the ministry of Jesus and his followers is confined, during his lifetime, to the Jewish people, while the mission to the gentiles begins only after his resurrection.[9] Luke, on the other hand, indicates that Jesus was concerned with gentiles during his lifetime, e.g., Samaritans and Syrians, and omits the Markan report in which Jesus initially declined to "take the [Jewish] children's bread and throw it to the [gentile] dogs" (Mark 7 : 24–30). The fact that Luke is known to omit other Markan material which he found offensive or incongruous leads to the suspicion that he may have treated some of the "Q" material similarly. One cannot, therefore, simply assign material that appears only in Matthew to this evangelist's inventiveness; especially is this the case where the Matthean material conflicts with Lukan interests. Consequently, it may be that the limitation of the mission to Israel was found in "Q," but omitted by Luke, rather than invented by Matthew. At any rate, Matt. 15 : 24 only makes explicit what is implied in the Markan version of the Story of the Greek or Syro-phoenician Woman, namely, that Jesus regarded his ministry as directed primarily, if not exclusively, to the Jewish people.

The Markan setting for the mission discourse likewise suggests that the twelve were to carry out their work only in the villages of Jesus' "own country" (Mark 6 : 1–7). It may be, in fact, that the Markan version contemplates a mission only in the immediate vicinity of Jesus' home (Capernaum) or, at most, Galilee. In any case, twelve would scarcely have been an adequate number of missionaries to send out to the whole world (even if allowance is made for the small size of the known world at that time), especially if the end events were expected in the near future. There is no reason to believe that either Jesus or the twelve carried on a ministry of preaching and exorcism outside of the territory of an-

8. See above, Chs. 3–6. Thus also Charles W. F. Smith, "Fishers of Men," *HTR* 52 (1959), 187–203. Cf. the Parables of the Harvest (Matt. 13 : 24–30, 37–43) and the Dragnet (13 : 47–50).
9. Matt. 15 : 24, 24 : 14, 28 : 19 f. But note Matt. 8 : 5–13 ("Q").

cient Israel. The reference to "Israel" in 10 : 23 does not compel the conclusion that the verse is secondary. It only expresses what otherwise is implicit.

The strongest support for the authenticity of the verse comes from the very theological difficulty it presents, not only to modern interpreters, but also to the early Church. The prophecy or assurance that the Son of man would come before the twelve had completed their mission was not realized. As H. P. Owens says, "Who would have invented a logion that was plainly unfulfilled?"[10] Matthew elsewhere accepts the Markan idea that the preaching mission to the gentiles must precede "the end" (Mark 13 : 10–13; Matt. 24 : 13 f., 28 : 19 f.). Why should he have invented a saying which conflicts with this understanding?[11] Although Matt. 10 : (16) 17–22 may well reflect the experience of early Christian communities (though not, necessarily, that of early Christian *missionaries*), this is not evidently the case in v. 23. We do not know of any such urgent mission through Israel on the part of the twelve in the post-Easter Church.[12] Matthew must have known that the twelve had completed their work—which, if not a mission, was confined to Israel![13]—and yet the Kingdom of God and Son of man had not come. Luke has elsewhere attempted to adjust the tradition in order to show that Jesus did not expect the immediate coming of the Kingdom after all, and had advised his followers accordingly.[14] That Luke should have omitted such a verse is not surprising. That Matthew should have preserved it is probably to be explained as an instance of his fidelity to the tradition that came to him from earlier times.[15]

Whether considered as a detached logion or, as seems more likely, a part of the earlier (possibly "Q") tradition as to Jesus' instructions to his followers on the occasion of their urgent mission of preaching and exorcism authorized and begun (if not completed)

10. "The Parousia of Christ in the Synoptic Gospels," *SJT* 12 (1959), 175 f. So also Schniewind, *Matthäus*, p. 131.

11. Thus also Tödt, *Son of Man*, pp. 90 f.

12. Despite Fuller, *Foundations*, p. 147. See Ferdinand Hahn, *Mission in the New Testament*, SBT no. 47 (Naperville, Ill., 1965), pp. 47–54.

13. Despite the "charge" of Matt. 28 : 19 f. See Gal. 2. Also Schmithals, *Paul and James*.

14. See below, Ch. 10.

15. Matthew's unbothered juxtaposition of Jesus' Davidic ancestry with the virgin birth story is another example.

during his lifetime, Matt. 10 : 23 may be considered authentic. Its meaning corresponds fairly precisely to that of other sayings in the synoptic gospels where Jesus proclaims or understands that the coming of the Kingdom of God and Son of man is near (Mark 1 : 15, 9 : 1, 13 : 30, and par.). That Jesus taught his disciples to pray for the coming of the Kingdom, and to proclaim to others its nearness is also well attested.[16] It is not surprising that this hope should have been preserved by the Church beyond the Apostolic Age. But it does not seem likely that the Church would have invented such sayings and attributed them to Jesus after the passing of the generation of his contemporaries. The Church's problem was to explain the fact that this earlier expectation had not been fulfilled.[17]

16. Matt. 6 : 10 = Luke 11 : 2; Matt. 10 : 7 = Luke 10 : 9, 11; Mark 13 : 32–37 and par.; Luke 12 : 32; 17:20–18:8.

17. E.g., Luke 19 : 11; Acts 1 : 7; John 21 : 22 f.; and, of course, II Pet. 3.

9

The Kingdom of God and the Parables

T HE MOST important study of this subject is still C. H. Dodd's *The Parables of the Kingdom*. Dodd proposes that in the ministry of Jesus "the Kingdom of God came," and that Jesus "used parables to enforce and illustrate the idea that the Kingdom of God had come upon men there and then."[1] This theory of "realized eschatology" has been taken over to varying degrees in subsequent studies of the parables, e.g., those of J. Jeremias, A. M. Hunter, and N. Perrin. Detailed criticism of this theory and exegesis of the parables would fill a separate volume. This chapter will simply review the synoptic parables[2] and note that they generally look for the coming of the Kingdom of God and events relating to it in the future.

For purposes of this review, the term "parable" will be used to indicate all stories, analogies, and images, not only those designated as "parables" by the evangelists or as "similitudes" by critics. The great majority of the parables have to do with the Kingdom of God, a fact which is not surprising considering that the imminence of the Kingdom was the central message of Jesus and his disciples as otherwise reported in the synoptic tradition. They do not describe the Kingdom of God as such,[3] but suggest some analogy between the action of one (or more) of the figures in the story and the kind of response Jesus' hearers should make in view of the prospective events.

Many parables clearly refer to the future coming of the Kingdom of God, Son of man, or Judgment, and call upon the hearer

1. 2d rev. ed. (New York, 1961), pp. 159 f.
2. Because of their problematic value as historical evidence, the parables in the *Gospel of Thomas* will not be considered here. But cf. such logia as 20, 22, 57, 76, 96–98, 107, 109. There are no parables in the Fourth Gospel.
3. Cf. Weiss, *Predigt*, pp. 10 f.

(or, from the standpoint of the evangelists, the reader) to respond now in such a way as to be ready when these decisive events do occur.

The parables of Hidden Treasure and the Pearl illustrate the point stated imperatively in Matt. 6 : 19–33: those who wish to enter the Kingdom must give up all other treasures for the sake of the one of surpassing worth, viz., the Kingdom itself (Matt. 13 : 44 f.). The same conception is implicit in the analogy of the Rich Man and a Camel (Mark 10 : 25 and par.). Those who now renounce all will then enter the Kingdom or "Age to come."[4] This choice between the Kingdom of God and all other goods also constitutes the thrust of the parable of the Marriage Feast (Matt. 22 : 1–5, 9–10) and the similar story of the Great Banquet (Luke 14 : 15–24).[5]

The parable of the Ten Maidens (Matt. 25 : 1–13) and Luke's similitude of the Waiting Men (12 : 35–38) emphasize the necessity of being continually prepared for the coming of the Kingdom,[6] a warning that recurs throughout the parabolic as well as nonparabolic teaching.

The parable of the Unmerciful Servant (Matt. 18 : 23–35) dramatizes the understanding implicit in the "Lord's Prayer," that only those are forgiven, hence ready for the coming of the Kingdom, who also forgive or have forgiven others (Matt. 6 : 12 = Luke 11 : 4a). Another "M" parable, the Laborers in the Vineyard, illustrates a related point, the freedom of God to admit to the Kingdom those who are summoned and respond as late as the eleventh hour (20 : 1–16). Admission to the Kingdom depends on one's

4. Mark 10 : 28–30 and par., esp. Matt. 19 : 28 and Luke 18 : 29 f.

5. The Matthean version reflects later Christian experience: vv. 6 f. intrusively allude to the fate of early Christian martyrs and the destruction of Jerusalem. Reference to "both bad and good" suggests the mixed populace of the church awaiting the Judgment: cf. Matt. 13 : 24–30, 47–50. Some interpreters hold that in these instances Matthew equates the Kingdom of Heaven with the Church. Possibly he does so regard the Kingdom of the Son of man (13 : 41), though that concept seems to refer to the future mixed company assembled for Judgment before the Son of man rather than to the Church of Matthew's time. In all of these instances, it is obvious that the decisive events—the Judgment, appearance of the Son of man, harvest, separation, close of the age, entering the Kingdom (banquet hall)—were understood by Matthew as future occurrences.

6. The Lukan setting (12 : 31 f.) indicates that the coming of the Kingdom is the question at hand, and the Son of man in the analogy of the Thief (12 : 39 f.) is the counterpart of the returning master in 12 : 35–38.

orientation toward God and man at the decisive moment when it (or the Son of man) comes, not upon previous debt or merit.

Numerous parables implicitly presuppose the future coming of the Kingdom as context, while concentrating upon the kind of behavior appropriate in the meantime for those who hope to enter it. The parable of the Talents or Pounds (Matt. 25 : 14–30 = Luke 19 : 12–27) warns of responsibility for that with which one has been entrusted. The eschatological future implicit in the eventual return of the master or nobleman is made explicit by Matthew (25 : 14, 30), while Luke places the parable where he does specifically in order to "explain" the prospective delay of the Kingdom's appearance (19 : 11). Matthew's version, too, anticipates some delay (25 : 19a). The instance of the Faithful and Wise Servant (Matt. 24 : 45–51 = Luke 12 : 42–46) similarly warns against failure to act responsibly in the interim occasioned by the master's delay. In both Matthew and Luke (thus, presumably, in "Q") this instance follows the explicit warning to be ready for the coming of the Son of man "at an hour you do not expect," which is joined to the image of the coming of the Thief (in the night) (Matt. 24 : 42–44 = Luke 12 : 39 f.). Several of these analogies parallel the Markan similitude of a Man Going on a Journey (13 : 33–37). The problem of delay is also a concern in the parable of the Unjust Judge (Luke 18 : 1–8): God will vindicate his people; the Son of man will come; but in the meantime the faithful should continue to pray—for the coming of the Kingdom, of course (cf. Matt. 6 : 10)—and not lose heart.

It is customary to refer the sayings which imply that the coming of the Kingdom or Son of man has been (or will be) delayed to the experience, and so, also, to the editorial hand, of the early community. Certainly the church did experience such a delay. That this was a problem is further evidence that Jesus and his companions had looked for these events at an early date. But it may well be that Jesus himself was puzzled by the delay in the appearance of the Kingdom or Son of man. He had taught his followers to hope and pray that it would come soon, and he and they had gone about proclaiming its nearness. But it did not come. Consequently, it is not simply to be assumed that references to delay are secondary.[7] And if some or all of them were, it would

7. See above, Ch. 8, and my article "Not the Season."

only indicate (what is apparent elsewhere) that the evangelists and the early communities they represent still awaited the coming of the Kingdom as a *future* event. Most of the parables, however, do not indicate any problem or prospect of delay. The analogy of the Accuser implies that one is already "on the way" to Judgment (Matt. 5 : 25 f. = Luke 12 : 57–59).

The parables peculiar to Luke do not ordinarily mention the Kingdom of God, and several of them are not described as parables. But they typically illustrate the kind of faith and life fitting for those who await fulfillment of the good news of the nearness of the Kingdom. The "parable" of the Good Samaritan is offered in response to the query of the lawyer (who wished to inherit eternal life, i.e., the Kingdom of God) who wanted to know whom he could exclude from the category "neighbor" (10 : 29–37). The parable of Rich Fool (12 : 13–21), like the anecdotes of the Unrighteous Steward (16 : 1–9) and the Rich Man and Lazarus (16 : 19–31), shows the futility of serving mammon, i.e., wealth or property; and the latter stories summon the hearer-reader to use what he has for the poor while there is still time, a theme common both to parables that refer explicitly to the Kingdom and to nonparabolic teaching.[8]

The analogy of the Lost Sheep (which Luke describes as a parable [15 : 3]) and the Lukan example of the Lost Coin (15 : 8–10) point to the ultimate importance of repentance.[9] There is already joy in heaven (where the Kingdom or Reign of God now obtains) over the sinner who repents, the lost which is found. Similarly, in the story of the Prodigal Son that immediately follows, the father's joy at the repentance or return of the profligate son represents the joy of the Heavenly Father at the finding of the lost, while the elder brother's complaint corresponds to the challenge of the laborers in the vineyard who had worked through the heat of the day (Matt. 20 : 11 f.). Although the Kingdom is not mentioned, the terms "lost" and "found" hint at the eschatological context elsewhere prominent in Luke: those who are "found" presumably are destined for a share in the coming Kingdom.

The parable of the Pharisee and the Publican (18 : 9–14) concludes the special Lukan parables with the threat and promise of

8. See above, p. 73, and my article "Friends by Unrighteous Mammon," *JAAR* 38 (1970), pp. 30–36.
9. So also the allusion to the fate of the Galileans and the Eighteen at Siloam (13 : 3, 5) and the parable of the Fig Tree (13 : 6–9).

future humiliation and exaltation—for those who now exalt and humble themselves, respectively. That this reversal of affairs is to take place in the Kingdom of God may be inferred from the location of the parable immediately after the eschatological sayings in 17:20–18:8, and from similar assurances and warnings in the Lukan Beatitudes (6 : 20–26).

The parable of the Four Soils (Mark 4 : 1–9 and par.) is linked to the "secret(s)" or "mystery" of the Kingdom of God by the evangelists. As it stands, its meaning is obscure, and exemplifies the Markan view that the parables were meant to be unintelligible to "those outside" (4 : 11 f.). The "explanation" (4 : 13–20 and par.) may be secondary, but at least gives the evangelists' understanding, which is that only those who renounce other cares and riches and withstand Satan and the expected tribulation (cf. Matt. 6 : 13) can hope to enter the Kingdom. Bringing forth fruit (Mark 4 : 8, 20) is suggestive of the harvest image for the Kingdom, and also of the yield of "talents" in the "Q" parable of that name. Since Satan is still operative (4 : 15 and par.), it is quite unlikely that the evangelists supposed that the Kingdom of God had as yet been established on earth. The Tree Bearing Good Fruit is another image suggestive of the way of life that should characterize the faithful (Matt. 7 : 16–20 and par.; cf. Luke 13 : 6–9), for only those who do the will of God shall enter the Kingdom (7 : 21).[10] Such also is the implication of the similitude of the Two Houses which closes the "Q" Sermon on the Mount (or Plain) (Matt. 7 : 24–27 = Luke 6 : 47–49).

The most vivid description, both of Judgment before the Son of man and of the kind of life required in the interim for those who are to inherit the Kingdom, is provided in Matt. 25 : 31–46. This is not, however, a "parable," but is reported simply as Jesus' account of what is to take place when the Son of man comes.

Three parables or similitudes of the Kingdom suggest (to some) a process of growth, culminating in fulfillment: the Seed Growing Secretly, the Mustard Seed, and the Leaven (Mark 4 : 26–29, 30–32, and par.; Matt. 13 : 33 = Luke 13 : 20 f.). Proponents of "realized eschatology" have made much of these parables. The question here is, in what manner is the Kingdom like the seed or leaven? Is the Kingdom present on earth, in the process of actual-

10. Thus also the parable of the Two Sons (Matt. 21 : 28–32).

izing itself here? Or is the analogue the miraculous result: the harvest, the great shrub, the transformation of the whole batch of dough? Both harvest and the great tree are traditional images for the Messianic Age.[11] Clearly this era had not yet begun. The transformation of the world was still in the future. It is improbable that Jesus or the evangelists thought in terms of modern theories of evolution. He, or they, may have thought the Kingdom present on earth in some hidden or incipient fashion. But it seems more likely that these parables were intended to give encouragement to his companions who, with him, were engaged in an urgent mission of preparation for the coming of the Kingdom. Despite appearances, their labors would bear fruit; the miracle would occur; God would establish His Kingdom on earth.[12]

If the meaning of these three parables ("of growth") is not certain, this uncertainty should not be taken as an excuse for overlooking the unmistakable meaning of the other parables of the Kingdom: that those who wish to enter the Kingdom of God must now act to make themselves ready, for it is coming soon.

11. Cf. Ezek. 17 : 22 ff., and my article "Not the Season," pp. 395–98.
12. So also, e.g., Martin Dibelius, *Jesus* (Philadelphia, 1949), pp. 66–68.

10

Special Features of the Synoptic Tradition

THE PASSAGES examined in the previous chapters come from all four of the synoptic "sources" or strata. In all these strata it is expected that the Kingdom of God and/or Son of man will soon come, and all refer to the conflict going on between Satan and the demons on one hand, and Jesus and his followers on the other.

Certain differences in emphasis appear, however, when the special characteristics of each source are examined. In some instances, these differences can be accounted for by referring to the history or situation of the communities where the gospels were composed, or to the particular concerns or style of the editor-authors.

One of the familiar peculiarities of Matthew's gospel is his preference for the expression "Kingdom of *heaven*." In earlier times this was thought to have some special significance *vis-à-vis* Kingdom of *God*. It is now recognized, however, merely as a circumlocution, i.e., a way of avoiding use of the divine name, a concern typical of Jewish and, to some extent, Christian piety then and since. In some cases, Matthew employs other circumlocutions—e.g., "life" (18 : 9), "Kingdom of my Father" (26 : 29). The fact that Matthew's usage is secondary may be seen by consulting the Gospel Parallels at numerous places where Luke follows Mark's reading "Kingdom of God," while Matthew simply changes "God" to "heaven" (e.g., at Mark 4 : 11, 30; 10 : 14, 15). Matthew evidently used the same procedure when following "Q" (e.g.: Matt. 5 : 3=Luke 6 : 20; Matt. 10 : 7=Luke 9 : 2; 10 : 9; Matt. 11 : 11= Luke 7 : 28). In two cases Matthew seems to have neglected to make the change (12 : 28, 19 : 24). The expression "Kingdom of God" also appears in 21 : 31, a pericope peculiar to Matthew. Here, possibly, he was following a "Q" reading omitted by Luke or, perhaps, some other source. In any case, it is apparent that for

Matthew "Kingdom of heaven" was only another way of saying "Kingdom of God": so also, for example, 6 : 10, 33; 13 : 43.

Another expression characteristic of Matthew is "consummation" or "end of the age" (*sunteleia* [*tou*] *aiōnos*). Apart from Heb. 9 : 26, it does not occur in the NT other than in Matthew, who presents it five times (13 : 39, 40, 49; 24 : 3; 28 : 20). Contrary to those interpreters who understand this to mean the consummation or completion *of the coming age* (i.e., Kingdom of God), it is quite clear that the expression means the end or completion *of the present age*. In the first three instances (13 : 39, 40, 49) it refers, specifically, to the time of the parousia of the Son of man and judgment, that decisive future complex of events which would separate the present age from the coming age, as well as the righteous (who would then enter the Kingdom) from the wicked (who would be excluded from it). In 24 : 3 "the close of the age" likewise is expected at the time of the "coming" of the Messiah–Son of man. In 28 : 20 the assurance is given that the risen Jesus will remain (on earth?) with his followers "all the days until" (*pasas tas hēmeras heōs*) the end of the age. The coming age, of course, would not have an end, since it would be the time of eternal life with the Messiah (e.g., Mark 10 : 30 and par.). The traditional Jewish distinction between the present age and the coming age appears in all three of the synoptic gospels;[1] the term *sunteleia* [*t.*] *aiōnos*, therefore, like Kingdom of Heaven, represents only a stylistic rather than conceptual peculiarity on Matthew's part.

Matthew, more than the other evangelists, emphasizes the decisive judgment that awaits mankind, and uses certain characteristic phrases to describe the fate of the condemned. The judgment is stressed in such "M" material as 12 : 36 f.; 13 : 24–30, 36–43, 47–50; and, of course, the description of the so-called Last Judgment, 25 : 31–46.[2] The righteous are to enter into "eternal life," i.e., the Kingdom of God (13 : 43, 25 : 46). Matthew twice uses a distinctive expression for those apparently destined for this favorable outcome: they are "sons of the Kingdom" (8 : 12, 13 : 38). Various typical phrases depict the fate of the condemned. They shall be ejected into "outer darkness" (8 : 12, 22 : 13, 25 : 30); or injected into the "furnace of fire" (13 : 42, 50; cf. 25 : 41). There—

1. E.g., Matt. 12 : 32; Mark 10 : 30 = Luke 18 : 30; Luke 20 : 34 f.
2. Matthew does not describe the scene as the "last" judgment, as if there were some earlier judgment.

wherever it may be—"there will be weeping and gnashing of teeth" (8 : 12; 13 : 42, 50; 22 : 13; 24 : 51; 25 : 30). In addition to 18 : 8–9 which is taken over from Mark, Matthew introduces six more references to "Gehenna" as the ultimate abode of sinners (5 : 22, 29, 30; 10 : 28; 23 : 15, 33).

Not all of these images or phrases are peculiar to Matthew. All of the sources or strata refer to the coming time of judgment. Mark speaks of Gehenna and unquenchable fire in prospect for the condemned (9 : 42–49), and "Q" of Gehenna (Matt. 10 : 28 = Luke 12 : 5) and the day of judgment when Capernaum will be brought down to Hades (Matt. 11 : 22 f. = Luke 10 : 15). The Markan admonition that the eschatological messengers should shake or wipe the dust of the impenitent cities from their feet[3] was probably understood either symbolically, as a prophetic gesture of condemnation (cf. Ezek. 4–5), or realistically, lest the missionaries should be injured or destroyed along with the soil of those doomed towns that still clings to them. The reference to "weeping and gnashing of teeth" at Matt. 8 : 12 has a parallel in Luke 13 : 28, the only place in the NT outside of Matthew where this expression is found, and here, probably, it should be attributed to "Q." Luke omits Mark's triple reference to "hell-fire" (Mark 9 : 43–49), possibly because he finds it distasteful, or because he does not wish to encourage those who might take such advice literally and mutilate themselves in order to improve their chances for entering the Kingdom of God. (Cf. Matt. 19 : 12.) It may be that Luke also preferred to omit the rest of the other references to Gehenna and "weeping and gnashing of teeth" because he found them objectionable (but cf. Luke 16 : 23 f.!). We cannot be certain whether Matthew emphasized this prospect, or whether Luke chose to de-emphasize it. However distasteful this idea may be to us in our enlightened (?) age, we cannot assume that Jesus himself objected to it. He may have regarded it as a matter already decided by God, as in Isa. 66 : 24. In any case, the idea that the condemned would suffer torment in Gehenna or Hades is not confined to Matthew's gospel, but appears in all four synoptic sources or strata.

Matthew stresses the role that Jesus or the Son of man will have in the judgment as judge. Some of the "M" traditions speak of Jesus' kingdom, or the Kingdom of the Son of man, as that intermediate era and area where he will preside in judgment over men

3. Mark 6 : 11, repeated in Matt. 9 : 14 f. = Luke 10 : 10–12.

(Matt. 13 : 41, 16 : 28, 20 : 21). The idea of the Kingdom of the Son of man or Messiah is not found explicitly in the two earliest strata, Mark and "Q."[4] It does, however, appear in certain "L" verses (Luke 22 : 30; 23 : 42; cf. 19 : 12–27). Whether the idea may be attributed to Jesus is in doubt. It was one of the tasks of the monarch in ancient Israel to judge his people, for there was no separate supreme judiciary under the monarchy (II Sam. 15 : 1–6). When judicial decisions were made by local officials, aggrieved parties could appeal to the king. The coming Davidic Messiah was expected to pronounce judgment, but unlike some kings Israel had known, he would give justice to the poor and meek (e.g., Isa. 11 : 1–5). Possibly Jesus spoke with a sense of messianic, and not only prophetic, authority when he assured the poor, meek, perse-cuted, and righteous that they would inherit the Kingdom (Matt. 5 : 3–12; cf. Luke 6 : 20–23). Or, it may be a special Matthean tendency: Matthew's Parable of the Marriage Feast has a king who pronounces eschatological judgment (22 : 13); and in his Description of the Separation (or "Last Judgment") the Son of man (25 : 31) is also described as "the King" (25 : 34, 40).

It is possible that the Matthean references to the Kingdom of the Son of man are simply another Matthean circumlocution, i.e., a way of avoiding writing "Kingdom of God." In that case the two ex-pressions would be equivalent (cf. Matt. 16 : 28 = Mark 9 : 1). On the other hand, in Matt. 13 : 41 the Kingdom of the Son of man seems to refer to the mixed company (world or church?) awaiting the harvest at the close of the age, and thus to the mixed assembly who are to come before the Son of man for judgment. Then, after the judgment, the righteous will enter the Kingdom *of God* (13 : 43). The idea that an interim reign of the Christ will give way, once evil has been overcome, to the Kingdom of God appears also in I Cor. 15 : 24–28.

Only Matthew tells that the angels who are to participate in the final separation or judgment belong to the Son of man (13 : 41, 16 : 27, 24 : 31). They are to perform the same function as in the Markan parallels—accompany the Son of man at the parousia, and "gather the elect." In the "M" Parable of the Weeds (13 : 41) they also throw the "weeds" (= the wicked) into the "furnace of fire." The angels are to function as bailiffs of the court.

4. It may well be implicit, however, in both: see Mark 8 : 38, 10 : 37–40, 13 : 26 f.; Matt. 7 : 21–23 = Luke 13 : 26 f.

A final peculiarity of Matthew's Gospel is the absence in it of any references (within the "M" material) to the future resurrection. Perhaps this is because Matthew wished to give no quarter to the despised Pharisees who believed in the resurrection. Or, perhaps, Matthew did not wish to add to the earlier tradition represented by Mark and "Q" which looked for the coming of the Son of man, judgment, and Kingdom so soon (within the present generation) that the question of resurrection was not existentially relevant. The "Q" tradition evidently contemplated only the resurrection of the dead of previous generations.[5] It is only in the "L" material and the Fourth Gospel that the fate of Christians who have died has become a problem.[6]

Several Markan traditions report that Jesus expected the Kingdom of God or Son of man to come soon (1 : 15), at the latest within "this generation," i.e., the lifetime of his contemporaries. This is stated explicitly in 13 : 30, and, in effect, in 8:38–9:1. It is sometimes argued that 9 : 1, which speaks of the coming of the Kingdom of God *with power* (*en dunamei*), implies that the Kingdom is already present *without* power. But Jesus and his followers expected the Kingdom of God and Son of man to come powerfully: heaven and earth would be transformed (13 : 26, 31; cf. Luke 17 : 24). The expectation that when the Kingdom comes, it will do so "in power" or powerfully, does not imply that it was already present without power or powerlessly.[7] Moreover, there is no evidence in Mark that Jesus thought the Kingdom of God present at all. According to Mark, Jesus' initial proclamation was that the Kingdom of God would soon come (1 : 15). He may have expected it to begin with his entrance into Jerusalem, but if so this hope was disappointed.[8] At the last supper he assured his followers (or vowed?) that he would yet drink wine (with them at the messianic table?) in the Kingdom of God (14 : 25). He warned the chief priests and members of the Sanhedrin that they (not their

5. See below, p. 91.
6. Outside the gospels, it was also noted as a problem: as early as Paul's time (I Cor. 15; I Thess. 4), and as late as II Pet. 3.
7. Dodd's reading of the verse—some will see (realize) that the Kingdom has already come—is refuted by Reginald H. Fuller, *The Mission and Achievement of Jesus*, SBT no. 12 (London, 1954), p. 27: "The decisive argument against this interpretation is that *oran* ("to see") is never used of intellectual perception."
8. See Hiers, "Not the Season," 394–400.

successors) would see the exalted Son of man coming with the clouds of heaven (14 : 62). After his death, one of his followers was still waiting for the Kingdom of God to come (15 : 43;[9] cf. Acts 1 : 6).

According to 13 : 32, not even "the Son" knows precisely the "day" or "hour." However, there is evidence elsewhere in Mark 13 of a later perspective. Vv. 7–29 present an apocalyptic schema, some items of which probably refer to events which had already taken place at the time the gospel (or possibly an earlier "little apocalypse") was composed: wars or the rising of nation against nation (7–8), persecution of the Christian community and testimony to Roman officials (9, 11), the gentile mission (10), and flight to the mountains (Pella?) in 14 ff. Some items were borrowed from the treasury of Jewish apocalyptic imagery that had been accumulating at least since the composition of Daniel. The main purpose of the schema seems to be to explain why the earlier expectation had not been fulfilled. The point in vv. 7–13 is that God had planned, and Jesus known, that there should be an initial stage or period of history in which Jesus' followers would have to deal with a hostile world; but they are not to be alarmed (7) or anxious (11), for "this must (*dei*)[10] take place" (7); however, it is only "the beginning of the birth pangs" (of the messianic age?) or "sufferings" (8). The "end" (*to telos*—not "the eschaton!"), however, is not yet. "First (*prōton*) the Gospel must (*dei*) be preached to all the gentiles" (10). In the meantime, Jesus' followers can survive, for the Holy Spirit will be with them (cf. the Johannine Paraclete), and "he who endures to the end (*eis telos*) will be saved" (13). In other words, the end would not come until the completion of the gentile mission (which here is assumed, though Mark contains no instruction by Jesus authorizing it). Nor would it come until after the Jewish war of 66–70 CE, if that is what is referred to in vv. 7–8a.

Then comes a second stage (14–23), the beginning of which is to be marked by the erection of the "desolating sacrilege" (which is probably based more on the visions of Daniel[11] than on any recent historical happening), a time of unprecedented "tribulation"

9. See Bauer, *Lexicon*, p. 719, "*prosdechomai*," 2b.
10. Cf. Dan. 2 : 28 LXX. If the LXX is echoed here, it is further evidence of the secondary character of the saying, since, so far as is known, Jesus did not speak Greek.
11. Dan. 9 : 27, 11 : 31, 12 : 11.

(*thlipsis*). During this period (as well as earlier—cf. 13 : 5 f.) false messianic pretenders or their prophets will come forth, but they must be ignored, for when the Son of man comes, it will not be a matter of minor "signs and wonders" (13 : 22). Instead, the *third* stage, the arrival of the Son of man, will be heralded or accompanied by unmistakable cosmic phenomena (13 : 24–27; cf. Luke 17 : 20 ff.). When *these* things take place, the faithful may know that the true Messiah–Son of man "is close upon the gates" (13 : 29).

It may be that Mark wrote when at least *some* of that generation had not yet passed away.[12] He uses the second person plural throughout most of the apocalypse (e.g., vv. 23, 29). But the impersonal "they" in v. 26, and also "the elect" in v. 22, suggest that Mark was trying to stretch the validity of the promises beyond the demise of the apostolic age. It is doubtful that he visualized the completion of the gentile mission within the lifetime of the apostolic generation (though the author of Col. 1 : 23 did!). It is possible, however, that he regarded this work as nearing completion, with Paul's preaching in Rome. Probably Mark himself was still living in the first of these three stages, near the end of the generation of Jesus' contemporaries. If so, the hope that the promise of salvation might yet be fulfilled in their lifetime would have been all the more precious. The warning to "take heed, watch and pray" was still a word for Mark's contemporaries, for no one could tell when the master of the house might come (13 : 33–37).

It is in Mark's gospel that the eschatological conflict between Satan and the demons, on the one hand, and the Spirit of God, Jesus, and his disciples, on the other, is most prominently set forth. This conflict, or series of conflicts, constitutes a substantial portion of the first nine chapters of Mark.[13] Matthew adds little to the ex-

12. Is Mark 9 : 1 an accommodation of an earlier expectation represented by 13 : 30? Or do both represent an accommodation of a still earlier hope implicit, for example, in Matt. 10 : 23 and Luke 19 : 11? See Erich Grässer, *Das Problem der Parusieverzögerung in den synoptischen Evangelien und in der Apostelgeschichte* (Berlin, 1960), esp. pp. 74 f., 128–37. Grässer maintains that Jesus unequivocally and consistently expected the coming of the Kingdom in the *near* future. He regards Mark 13 : 30 and 9 : 1 as words of consolation originating in the early Christian community, in effect: even if the Kingdom has been delayed, it still can come in this generation. Marxsen's thesis as to Mark's setting and interest, if questionable in other respects, is correct in proposing that this evangelist looked for the coming of the Kingdom of God / Son of man at any time.

13. See above, esp. Ch. 5, and Robinson, *Problem of History in Mark.*

orcism or Satan narratives. Aside from doubling the number of demons or demoniacs on two occasions in order to heighten the miraculous effect, he contributes only the Parable of the Tares (see esp. 13 : 38 f.). Luke adds new (or otherwise unknown) material at 8 : 2; 10 : 17–20; 13 : 16; and 22 : 3, 31. The "Q" stratum has three additional exorcism episodes or sayings.[14] Neither Matthew nor Luke attempts to demythologize Satan or the demons, but the warfare waged by Jesus and his followers against the household of Satan seems less obvious in their gospels, mainly because they include more traditions concerning Jesus' teaching or sayings than does Mark, which is relatively more devoted to narrative. Exorcism traditions appear in all strata of the synoptic gospels, but there are none in the Fourth Gospel,[15] a fact which may be related to the demythologizing tendencies of this evangelist.

Luke adds several sayings about the future coming of the Kingdom of God (10 : 11; 19 : 11; 21 : 31; and 22 : 16, 18).[16] Two of these, 19 : 11 and 21 : 31, explain that Jesus did *not* expect the Kingdom to come immediately; only after certain subsequent events had transpired would it be near. Luke omits the saying at Mark 13 : 32, probably because he understands that Jesus *did* know when the Kingdom was coming, and, moreover, had undertaken to correct his followers' expectation, afterwards obviously erroneous, that it would come in the immediate future (thus also Acts 1 : 7). Nevertheless, the Lukan Jesus assures his "little flock" that God will give *them* the Kingdom (12 : 32).

The "L" tradition, like the "M" tradition, includes a few references to the Kingdom of the Messiah or Son of man (Luke 22 : 30, 23 : 42; cf. 19 : 15). All of these sayings suggest an idea which appears also in the Acts "speeches" and Paul's letters: that Jesus received the office of Christ, Lord, or Son of man only after his death and resurrection.[17] In Luke 22 : 69, unlike its parallels, Jesus

14. Matt. 9 : 32 f. = 12 : 22 f. = Luke 11 : 14; Matt. 12 : 27 f. = Luke 11: 19 f.; Matt. 12 : 43–45 = Luke 11 : 24–26.

15. Satan, however, is still operative in the Fourth Gospel (13 : 27; cf. 10 : 12, 28 f.; 12 : 31; 17 : 15; and I John, *passim*); and Jesus is still accused of being possessed by a demon (10 : 20 f.).

16. See above, Ch. 2, note 4. In that chapter it is argued that Luke 17 : 20 f. also belongs in this category.

17. Acts 2 : 22–36, 3 : 12–21; Rom. 1 : 3 f.; Phil. 2 : 9 f. See J. A. T. Robinson, "The Most Primitive Christology of All?" in his *Twelve New Testament Studies*, pp. 139–53.

tells the members of the Sanhedrin that "from now on the Son of man shall be seated at the right hand of the power of God."[18] Here Luke was evidently 'concerned to change an unfulfilled prophecy (that the members of the Sanhedrin would, soon or late, live to see the parousia of the Son of man) into one which could have been fulfilled, namely, the assession of the Son of man in his heavenly Kingdom. Perhaps all of the Lukan references to the Kingdom of the Son of man were intended to show that Jesus had, after all, entered into his Kingdom or kingly power—in heaven— despite the failure of the (premature) hope on the part of his disciples that they would soon see it come on earth.

In any case, the "L" tradition contains a variety of responses to what must have become a serious problem by the time Luke's gospel was written: that most if not all of the first Christians had died before the coming of the Kingdom of God and Son of man. What was and would be their fate?

Luke 20 : 34–36 contains one or two (possibly conflicting) answers to this question. Instead of saying that there will be no marriage among those risen from the dead (as in Mark 12 : 25 = Matt. 22 : 30), Luke, following perhaps the example if not also the teaching of Paul (cf. I Cor. 7 : 7–9, 38b), reports Jesus as having said that *now* there is to be no more marrying among those who aspire to the resurrection and life in the coming age. Mark and Matthew have it that *then* men will live, in this respect, as the angels do already. Luke proposes that men are already "equal to the angels" and so should live like them *now*. It is not clear here whether it was expected that the "sons of the resurrection" would still have to die and be raised, or whether they had, so to speak, already been born of the resurrection, so that they were now exempt from death: "for they cannot die any more."[19] A similar am-

---

18. Cf. Mark 14 : 62. Luke evidently did not recognize that "Power" in Mark is a circumlocution for "God," and so has the redundant and obscure expression "right hand of the power of God." J. A. T. Robinson, who leans heavily toward realized eschatology, prefers to think the Lukan version primary and the others secondary—*Jesus and His Coming* (Nashville, 1957).

19. Shakespeare and Freud would have found Luke's version fascinating. Possibly some recollection of the "L" verse (or I Cor. 7) lay behind Kierkegaard's rejection of Regina, which, however, he tried agonizingly to justify by reference to the willingness of the (married and subsequently remarried) patriarch Abraham to sacrifice his son Isaac (*Fear and Trembling*). Probably what Luke meant was that since death would not annul marriage for those already immortal (cf. I Cor. 7 : 39a), they should remain single in order to

biguity appears in the Johannine saying ". . . he who believes in me, though he die, yet shall he live, and whoever lives and believes in me shall never die" (John 11 : 25 f.). The ambiguity may arise, in part, out of the fact that while many Christians had died by the middle of the fourth quarter of the first century—probably all of the first generation, in fact—the belief continued that some would live to see the parousia of Christ and enter into the final bliss without having to die and then be raised again first (cf. John 21 : 20–23).

The term "sons of the resurrection," found only in Luke, may have been coined in the early Church as a designation for those believers who had died. They would need to be raised from the dead before they could enter the Kingdom of God.[20] Perhaps Luke expected that only the righteous would participate in the resurrection. The Lukan Jesus speaks of "the resurrection of the just" (14 : 14), but says nothing about the resurrection of the unrighteous (cf. John 5 : 28 f.). Here, again, Luke may share a Pauline view, for Paul speaks only of the resurrection of the "dead in Christ." Perhaps for Luke the "resurrection of the just" made any future judgment superfluous for them. The only reference to the future judgment in the "L" material has to do with the one which those who are still alive must undergo (21 : 36). When the Son of man comes, God will vindicate those in whom the Son of man finds faith (18 : 7 f.). Luke omits the references to Gehenna and hell fire at Mark 9 : 43–48, but does include from "Q" a reference to Gehenna (12 : 5), the destruction of Capernaum in Hades (10 : 15), and one of the allusions to "weeping and gnashing of teeth" (13 : 28).

A number of "L" traditions suggest that a person may enter Paradise (or Hades) immediately after death. In this case, also, a future resurrection and judgment would be unnecessary. The most obvious instance of this understanding is in the Story of the Rich Man and Lazarus (16 : 19–31). It may also be implicit in 12 : 20, 16 : 9, and 20 : 36. Jesus' reassurance to the "criminal" who was being executed with him (23 : 43) is a special problem. If authentic, did it mean that Jesus expected that "this day"—the same

avoid transgressing the thought, now on the way to doctrine, that in the coming age there would be no more marriage.

20. Cf. Paul's expression, "those who have fallen asleep," and his expectation that some (including himself) would still be alive at the parousia: I Cor. 15 : 51 f.; I Thess. 4 : 13–18.

day as his execution—he would come in his Kingdom (v. 42), i.e., the Kingdom of God would come? More likely, *Luke* understood it to mean that this day Jesus would come *into* his Kingdom (*eis tēn basileian sou*). Paradise is evidently understood here as a synonym for the Kingdom in heaven which Jesus was about to enter. Elsewhere in Luke, as we have seen, the evangelist understands that Jesus' Kingdom began (in heaven) following his death and resurrection. Here Luke seems to understand Jesus to have meant that both he and the believing "criminal" would enter, immediately upon death, into Paradise, namely, the Heavenly Kingdom of the Messiah.[21]

The idea that some of the righteous might enter Paradise immediately, without having to wait for the resurrection, may go back to earlier Jewish tradition; Jesus himself may have shared this belief. But since these traditions appear only in Luke, it is conceivable that they represent a response to the problem that already troubled the churches in Paul's time: What becomes of believers who have died and those who may yet die before the parousia? Must they wait for the resurrection before they can enter into the Kingdom of God, or in the meantime, may they enter, on death, the Kingdom of the Messiah, as it was believed Jesus himself had done? The question about the fate of the believer must have become more serious the longer the parousia was delayed. The Fourth Evangelist, of course, answered it with the assurance that believers (who are baptized, or partake of the body of Christ) already have eternal life.[22]

At several points, Luke addresses himself to the problem that the Kingdom of God had not yet come (despite traditions that Jesus had proclaimed its nearness, and the expectation of the earlier apostles).[23] Luke simply omits the account of Jesus' preaching at Mark 1 : 15, and instead uses the more general summary "preaching the good news of the Kingdom of God" (4 : 43) which avoids saying when the Kingdom might be expected. Luke's Jesus

21. How this thought is to be reconciled with the tradition of Jesus' resurrection after two or three days or with the Lukan ascension tradition (Acts 1 : 3, 9–11) is another problem. Cf. Matt. 28 : 20, and I Cor. 15 : 6–8.

22. John 3 : 5, 15, 16, 36; 4 : 14; 5 : 25; 6 : 27–33, 50, 53–58. But cf. 5 : 26–29, 6 : 40b, and 12 : 48 which speak of a future resurrection and judgment. Perhaps the earlier beliefs were not entirely forgotten in the days of the Fourth Evangelist.

23. This may have been one of the questions about which Luke wished to set the record straight (in "an orderly account"): 1 : 3 f.

attempts to correct the disciples' expectation that the Kingdom was near (19 : 11; Acts 1 : 6–8), and warns against false prophets or messiahs who make such a claim (21 : 8).

In Luke's time, the Kingdom still had not come. Several decades had passed since the days of Jesus. How should this delay be accounted for? Luke follows Mark in detailing certain stages of history that must first run their course. In 21 : 9 he notes that there must first be wars and tumults. Probably Luke understood this to mean the Jewish war of 66–70 C.E., which was not simply a rumor (cf. Mark 13 : 7) but a matter of history. Luke goes on to state that the fall of Jerusalem does not yet mark the end of history, but only the end for Jerusalem (21 : 20–24c), for still "the times of the gentiles" (i.e., the gentile mission) must be fulfilled. History, as Luke knew, had continued to go on twenty or thirty years after the fall of Jerusalem. Luke changes Jesus' warning to the Sanhedrin that they will see the parousia (Mark 14 : 62) into the doctrine of Jesus' assession or entrance into His Kingdom. Luke knew, of course, that the members of the Sanhedrin who had condemned Jesus sixty or seventy years previously had perished without witnessing his vindication.

Contrary to Conzelmann, however, who thinks that Luke's purpose was to defer the time of the parousia to the distant future, Luke is not consistent in his elimination or transformation of the imminent hope and expectation. Luke preserves Jesus' assurances that his followers would live to see the Kingdom of God (9 : 27, 21 : 32), adds that God would vindicate them (i.e., bring the Kingdom and Son of man) "speedily" (17:20–18:8; cf. 12 : 32), and retains the substance of the disciples' message that the Kingdom has come near (10 : 9, 11).

Why this inconsistency in Luke? In the first place, Luke should be given some credit for trying to do what he claims: to report accurately the tradition that had come to him. One need be only slightly familiar with the OT to be aware that inconsistencies often are preserved out of respect for the sacred tradition. We have grown so accustomed to the form-critical assumption that traditions were manufactured wholesale by the Church that we hardly any longer think it conceivable that an evangelist might have passed along a tradition because it came down to him on what he believed to be good authority. But there is another consideration. The message that the Kingdom of God and parousia were near was still existentially relevant to the Church in Luke's day.[24] To be sure, with the exception of 18 : 8, Luke does not stress the imminence of the Kingdom in the traditions peculiar to his gospel. But that he expected the Kingdom of God and Son of man to come at some time in the future is incontestable. It is unlikely that he visualized the continuation of history for nineteen more centuries. That history has continued is our problem (and opportunity), not Luke's.

Luke undertook to show that the earlier idea that the Kingdom of God should have come already was incorrect and out of kilter with both the divine plan and Jesus' own understanding of that plan. But he preserved the traditions which spoke of its imminence along with those which anticipated its coming in a somewhat more remote future, for Luke himself believed and was concerned to assure his fellow-believers that the Kingdom and Son of man would, indeed, come. They had not yet come, but since, *in Luke's time* they could come at any time, men must be ready at all times.[25] In the meantime, Luke's special concern was not with a doctrine of history or eschatology, but with showing both gentile and Hellenistic-Jewish-Christians that Jesus, the Messiah of the Jews, was also (if not especially) their "Lord" as well, and with showing gentile nonbelievers that this new religion was "the Way" for them too. When the "times of the gentiles" were completed, the Kingdom would then come.[26]

The "Q" tradition contains two explicit references to the future messianic banquet. One is Matt. 8 : 11 = Luke 13 : 28 f. The Lukan version mentions that not only the patriarchs, but "all the prophets" will be seen at table in the Kingdom of God. Whether it was understood that they were there already, or that they must first be raised from the dead, is not indicated. The other reference is the Parable of the Marriage Feast (Matt. 22 : 1–10) or the Story of the

24. Cf. the recurrent "this day" in Deut. 5–11. One might also think of the way in which "Bible prophecies" have been understood as intended primarily (if not exclusively) for the interpreter's generation.

25. Luke 12 : 35–48; Acts 2 : 38–47, 3 : 19–21, 14 : 21 f. Note also Acts 17 : 30 f. Since the mission to the gentiles was well along in Luke's time, the "fixed day" for the parousia and judgment might come at any time. See the careful study by Fred O. Francis, "Eschatology and History in Luke–Acts," *JAAR* 37 (1969), 49–63.

26. Luke 21 : 24b. Cf. Rom. 9–11. Matt. 28 : 19 f. also implies that the gentile mission would precede the close of the Age.

Great Banquet (Luke 14 : 16–24). Matthew's version reflects his preoccupation with the condemnation of the wicked (and also, probably a common Christian theory as to why Jerusalem was destroyed),[27] while Luke's focuses, characteristically, upon the salvation of the poor and afflicted. In each case, the wedding hall or banquet serves as an image or symbol for the promised salvation in the Kingdom of God.

Another special feature of "Q" is that it presents three separate sets of sayings with regard to the fate, at the judgment, of Jewish towns or the present generation of Jews compared to that of various gentile cities and persons of antiquity. The fate of the towns (of Israel) is contrasted, unfavorably, with that of the two most wicked cities of "history," Sodom (and Gomorrah) (Matt. 10 : 15= Luke 10 : 12). The Galilean cities of Chorazin, Bethsaida, and Capernaum are promised a less tolerable fate than that in store for the Phoenician cities Tyre and Sidon (Matt. 11 : 21–23=Luke 10 : 13–15; cf. Isa. 23, Ezek. 26, and Zech. 9 : 3 f.). Finally, the men of Nineveh and the queen of the South (Sheba) will arise at the judgment and condemn this present evil generation (Matt. 12 : 38–42=Luke 11 : 29–32). Presumably the present generation would not need to arise, since it would still be alive. Such is the understanding in another "Q" tradition at any rate (Matt. 23 : 36= Luke 11 : 50, 51). Matt. 10 : 15 = Luke 10 : 12 presupposes the resurrection of the dead from the ruins of the long-defunct cities of Sodom and Gomorrah. This may also be implicit in the Tyre and Sidon saying. Probably none of these sayings was intended to answer speculative questions as to the fate of the dead of antiquity, or to argue for "universalism" as against Jewish (or Christian) "particularism." Rather, as with other traditions attributed to Jesus, they were meant as a last summons to repentance—if possible—in the time that remains before the judgment.[28]

The "Q" tradition includes one saying that could be read to mean that Jesus thought that the Kingdom of God had arrived— Matt. 12 : 28 = Luke 11 : 20, where the verb form *ephthasen* ("has come upon") appears;[29] but "Q" also contains the message the disciples were to proclaim on their urgent mission (to Israel)—that

27. Cf. Luke 19 : 41–44.
28. See such other "Q" traditions as Matt. 5 : 25 f. = Luke 12 : 57–59; Matt. 7 : 24–27 = Luke 6 : 47–49; and the "L" sayings in Luke 13 : 1–9.
29. See above, however, Ch. 3.

the Kingdom of God had come *near* (*ēngiken*) (Matt. 10 : 7 =
Luke 10 : 9[11]). There are no "Q" traditions about any gentile
mission, let alone as prerequisite to the coming of the Kingdom. It
is also in "Q" that the prayer for the coming (not "completion")
of the Kingdom of God is found (Matt. 6 : 10 = Luke 11 : 2), as
well as the "Beatitudes," which promise a future recompense in
the Kingdom of God to the (righteous) poor among Jesus' hearers
who are now afflicted.[30]

Jesus is portrayed in "Q" as the one who will preside as judge in
the judgment (Matt. 7 : 21–23 = Luke 13 : 26 f.). And, according
to "Q" sayings, punishment in Hades (Matt. 11 : 23 = Luke 10 : 15)
or Gehenna (Matt. 10 : 28 = Luke 12 : 5) awaits the unrighteous
or unbelievers. Perhaps some of the other Matthean sayings to this
effect come from "Q" also: we do not know how many of them
Luke omitted, or which Matthew invented or culled from other
sources.

Although each of the synoptic strata has its own characteristic
images, concepts, or emphases, the basic understanding of history
is the same in all of them. Jesus and his followers were living in the
last days of the present age. There was still work to be done,
namely, proclaiming that the Kingdom of God had come near, and
casting out demons. Men should repent and believe in God. Jesus'
own followers should "watch," i.e., be faithful at all times also, for
soon the Son of man would come, men would be judged, and the
faithful-righteous would enter the Kingdom of God, while the im-
penitent-unresponsive would suffer torment or destruction in Gehenna.

30. Matt. 5 : 3–12 = Luke 6 : 20–23. Cf. Matt. 6 : 19–21 = Luke 12 : 33 f.
For further analysis of the basically eschatological traditions in "Q," see Kee,
Jesus in History, pp. 76–102.

11

Eschatology, Terminology, and the Futurity of the Kingdom

INTERPRETATION of the eschatological beliefs of Jesus and the early Church has been complicated by the desire of many interpreters to find a Jesus who substantiates their own philosophical or theological commitments. Luke 17 : 20 f. does not support the view that Jesus or Luke thought the Kingdom of God somehow already present; rather, when the Kingdom comes, there will be no mistake about it. The *ephthasen* saying of Matt. 12 : 28 = Luke 11 : 20 and the *biazetai* saying of Matt. 11 : 12 (cf. Luke 16 : 16) *may* mean that Jesus thought the Kingdom of God present in conflict with the forces of evil which still governed the earth; but the more likely reading is that by the power of the Holy Spirit, Jesus and his followers were overcoming the demons (and thus Satan), thereby preparing for the time when God's rule would be established on earth. Mark 3 : 27 indicates, similarly, that Jesus was binding the demons, working toward Satan's ultimate defeat, and "plundering" or "loosing" his victims, freeing them for the "harvest" or salvation in the coming Kingdom of God.

In Luke 10 : 17–20, Jesus tells of his prophetic vision of Satan's final defeat, a vision possibly inspired by the present victories over the demons. The saying at Matt. 11 : 11 = Luke 7 : 28 points to the surpassing worth of life in the Kingdom: there and then, the lowliest member of the Kingdom will exceed (in perfection of life or blessing) even the greatest of men here and now in the present age. Matt. 10 : 23 accords with other traditions to the effect that Jesus expected the Kingdom of God and Son of man to come in the near future. The parables for the most part clearly demonstrate Jesus' belief that the Kingdom of God would come in the future, and that men should now prepare for its coming if they wished to enter it then. Examination of the synoptic sources shows that all literary strata look to the future as the time when the Son of man will be revealed, the Judgment will take place, and the Kingdom of God will come.

Analysis of the precise character of the eschatological beliefs of Jesus and the early communities has been complicated by a high degree of semantic confusion, if not obfuscation. Certain writers introduce a profusion of arbitrary (or anachronistic) distinctions, attributing these freely to Jesus himself. J. Jeremias, for example, says that Jesus proclaimed the arrival of the "Messianic" or "New Age," but expected the Kingdom of God to come in the future.[1] G. E. Ladd's account is thoroughly confusing. He proposes to distinguish between "the messianic salvation" (= "the Kingdom of God") which is present and "the new aeon," which is still future. "The new age of salvation" is present; the "old order" or "age of the law and the prophets" is over; nevertheless, the "old aeon" or "old age" still continues.[2] Neither Jeremias nor Ladd makes any effort to ground this proliferation of nomenclature in the synoptic material, or even to define these various terms with reference to one another.

Writers too numerous to mention attribute to Jesus (or the early communities or evangelists) an understanding that the Kingdom of God was "dawning" or "breaking in" (*anbrechen*), or had already done so; that the "shift of aeons" was now taking place, or had already occurred; that the Kingdom of God was "proleptically" present; that its "powers" were operative in his ministry; that its "completion" or "consummation," however, was still to take place in the future. Such terms are repeated as if they represented the assured results of NT research. None of them, however, appears anywhere in the synoptic tradition.[3]

The same is true of the term "the eschaton." The noun *to eschaton* is used only adverbially in the NT, never as a substantive designating "the end" or the Kingdom of God. Nevertheless, it is employed even by such writers as W. G. Kümmel and H. Conzelmann as a synonym for "Kingdom of God."[4] Such Biblical expressions as "the last days" or "the last times" are, themselves, ambigu-

1. *Parables*, pp. 149–53, 225–29.
2. *Jesus and the Kingdom*, pp. 191–201.
3. Nor do such common expressions as "the last judgment" or "the second coming" of Christ.
4. E.g., Kümmel, *Promise and Fulfilment*, p. 64; Conzelmann, *Theology of St. Luke*, p. 119n1.

ous. Do these refer to the last days *of the present age,* or to *the coming age itself?* Most writers seem to be unaware of this fundamental question or distinction, and many simply assume that if a phenomenon of the *last days* is thought to be present—e.g., the healing of the sick, or the coming of Elijah—it follows that the *Kingdom of God* is also present. But in those places where *to telos* ("the end," or "limit") is used with reference to the times, it clearly refers to the future end of the present age (Matt. 10 : 22; Mark 13 : 7, 13). This is the case also with the Matthean expression *hē sunteleia tou aiōnos* ("the consummation of the age"). The adjectival form *eschatos* ("last") surprisingly does not appear in the synoptic strata with reference to the end of the present age or the coming of the coming age.[5] Luke uses the expression "in the last days" once (Acts 2 : 17), where, as in Joel 2 : 28–32, he refers to the restoration of prophecy to Israel, a phenomenon which was to *precede* the time of judgment and salvation (Joel 2 : 31 f.=Acts 2 : 20–21). In II Tim. 3 : 1, II Pet. 3 : 3, I John 2 : 18, and Jude 18, the reference is clearly to the last days of the *present* age (so also in *Test. Issachar* 6 : 1). Such is probably implied also in Heb. 1 : 2 and I Pet. 1 : 20. In James 5 : 3, as in John 12 : 48, it refers to the future time of judgment.

Our derivative term "eschatology" should therefore be used with care. An "eschatological" phenomenon may be one that belongs in the coming age or Kingdom of God (e.g., the messianic banquet), or it may be one that marks the transition or border between the ages—the coming or parousia of the Son of man, the resurrection, or the judgment. Or it may be one which was to take place in the last days of the present age, *near,* but not *at* its end (e.g., the coming of Elijah, the task of exorcism, and the preaching of repentance). There was, of course, no single apocalyptic program common to all Jewish or Christian writers of the Biblical and intertestamental period. But we should not make matters worse by mixing everything together into a general "eschatological" pot pourri. It might be useful to introduce some further analytical categories, e.g., a distinction between "ultimate" eschatological phenomena or events, "border" events, and "penultimate" phenomena. But we should not attribute our analytical categories to Jesus or

5. It is used several times in the Fourth Gospel with respect to the future day of *resurrection* and once for the future *judgment* (12 : 48). See Bauer, *Lexicon,* p. 314.

the Church tradition. Jesus was not a proponent of "realized" or any other kind of "eschatology."

Our exegesis of the several verses or pericopes studied may be inadequate or even incorrect at certain points. Yet it is significant that such seemingly difficult or obscure passages as Matt. 11 : 11, 11 : 12, and Luke 17 : 20 f. become intelligible when the eschatological beliefs of Jesus and his contemporaries, elsewhere evidenced in the various traditions, are taken into account.[6]

There can be no doubt that Jesus and the evangelists looked for the future actualization of the decisive "last" events: the coming or manifestation of the Son of man, the judgment of living (and resurrected dead?), and the coming of the Kingdom of God or coming age. That this certainty has played but little part in contemporary exegesis and theology can be attributed primarily to the dogmatic or philosophical interests (or aversions) of the "doers" of exegesis and theology. It is only quite recently that these "futuristic" beliefs are coming to be recognized as something other than a primitive Jewish and early Christian absurdity to be disposed of quickly and, if possible, quietly.[7]

The dominant hypothesis—that Jesus regarded the Kingdom as both future *and* somehow present—is now called into question. It is *possible* that Jesus spoke, on one or two occasions, of the Kingdom as present in his (and his disciples') struggle against the dominion (and minions or demons) of Satan. But it is by no means certain that Jesus thought the Kingdom present in this or any other sense. We should not try to force consistency of thought upon Jesus merely because we value coherence, or because we fail to understand the complexity of his particular understanding of the matter. But we should also avoid thrusting inconsistency upon him because of our own dogmatic preferences. It is significant that advocates of "realized" *and* "futuristic" eschatology generally end by eliminating the future expectation or its significance altogether— e.g., A. Harnack, A. N. Wilder, J. A. T. Robinson, N. Perrin, and

---

6. Such is the case also with Mark 11 : 12–14 and Luke 16 : 9. See my articles "Not the Season for Figs" and "Friends by Unrighteous Mammon," cited previously.

7. See Jürgen Moltmann, *Theology of Hope* (New York, 1967), esp. pp. 37 ff. Also Leander E. Keck, "Apocalyptic and the New Testament," unpublished paper (Nashville, 1968).

even R. Bultmann, in his exposition of the meaning of the "mythology."

The Kingdom of God was not yet "realized" (or actualized) on earth, so far as Jesus and the evangelists were concerned, if we can trust the preponderance of unambiguous synoptic evidence on this point. Yet Jesus did, evidently, believe that certain "eschatological" phenomena which we may call of penultimate character were already taking place during his lifetime—most notably the work of preparing the earth (at any rate, Israel) for the coming of the Kingdom by preaching its nearness and the need for repentance, and by exorcising or "binding" the demons.

Although "eschatology" and "the Kingdom of God" are commonly taken as equivalent terms—whether for dogmatic reasons, or because the synoptic evidence is ignored—the two are not the same. From the standpoint of the historical Jesus and the evangelists, certain "eschatological" events were understood to have taken place during and in connection with his ministry. But the balance of probability rests with the conclusion that neither the historical Jesus nor the synoptic evangelists believed that the Kingdom of God had come. As with the manifestation of the Son of man, the Judgment, and the Resurrection, they awaited its arrival in the future, and thought, hoped, prayed, and lived accordingly.

Index of Primary Citations

99

NEW TESTAMENT

Index

UNIVERSITY OF FLORIDA MONOGRAPHS

Humanities

No. 1: *Uncollected Letters of James Gates Percival*, edited by Harry R. Warfel

No. 2: *Leigh Hunt's Autobiography: The Earliest Sketches*, edited by Stephen F. Fogle

No. 3: *Pause Patterns in Elizabethan and Jacobean Drama*, by Ants Oras

No. 4: *Rhetoric and American Poetry of the Early National Period*, by Gordon E. Bigelow

No. 5: *The Background of The Princess Casamassima*, by W. H. Tilley

No. 6: *Indian Sculpture in the John and Mable Ringling Museum of Art*, by Roy C. Craven, Jr.

No. 7: *The Cestus. A Mask*, edited by Thomas B. Stroup

No. 8: *Tamburlaine, Part I, and Its Audience*, by Frank B. Fieler

No. 9: *The Case of John Darrell: Minister and Exorcist*, by Corinne Holt Rickert

No. 10: *Reflections of the Civil War in Southern Humor*, by Wade H. Hall

No. 11: *Charles Dodgson, Semeiotician*, by Daniel F. Kirk

No. 12: *Three Middle English Religious Poems*, edited by R. H. Bowers

No. 13: *The Existentialism of Miguel de Unamuno*, by José Huertas-Jourda

No. 14: *Four Spiritual Crises in Mid-Century American Fiction*, by Robert Detweiler

No. 15: *Style and Society in German Literary Expressionism*, by Egbert Krispyn